WORTH IT

WORTH IT

THE PATH TO AN MBA . . . AND BEYOND

Inspiring stories about young Brazilian graduates who pursued a master's in business administration in the United States and how they managed to take their careers to the next level.

Ricardo Betti

and

Ricardo Filho

Translated by Vanessa Blatt Rossi

iUniverse, Inc.
Bloomington

WORTH IT
The Path to an MBA ... and Beyond

iUniverse books may be ordered through booksellers or by contacting:

iUniverse
1663 Liberty Drive
Bloomington, IN 47403
www.iuniverse.com
1-800-Authors (1-800-288-4677)

ISBN: 978-1-4620-4412-2 (sc)
ISBN: 978-1-4620-4413-9 (hc)
ISBN: 978-1-4620-4414-6 (ebk)

Library of Congress Control Number: 2012905563

Printed in the United States of America

iUniverse rev. date: 05/10/2012

Contents

Foreword

The Achiever of Dreams . . .

I enjoy philosophy. I am, however, frustrated by knowing so little of the vast sweep of human thought. I am always fighting with my schedule, looking for time to devote to the subject. After all, the point of philosophy is to help us live better, clearer lives. In knowledge and self-knowledge, the fears brought by the darkness of ignorance fade. Where there is knowledge, there is light.

One of my favorite philosophers was a crucial thinker of the modern era: Immanuel Kant. The great German philosopher lived between 1724 and 1804 and asserted, "The intelligence and knowledge a man possesses can be measured by the amount of uncertainty he is capable of withstanding."

A new view, such as that provided by this book, is, for me, fertile ground for uncertainty. Consequently, reading it provided reflection and growth. Whenever I come across something truly new, I take a moment to digest my own ignorance. Sometimes I have to give up my convictions. "How is it that I never thought of that before?" is one of the questions that I often ask myself.

We all have lots to read every day. It seems that the hours go by and books remain unread too often. Selectivity is fundamental: we have to decide before we begin to read what deserves to be read. But, with so many new things to read out there, especially on the Internet, the question is, how do we evaluate the new, the unknown? The knowledge that we cannot read everything causes the distressing feeling that we have missed something important, perhaps the best part.

For those who have not yet learned to deal with so much information, it may be more of a hindrance than a convenience. In fact, more information adds very little—what we need is more knowledge.

Knowledge clearly serves two purposes: to be shared and to create value. Knowledge that resides within the individual, which is not shared with others, has little value. Only when it is exposed to criticism can it be modified, can it evolve and become immune to obsolescence. Moreover, knowledge has to be used to generate value for us, our families, our businesses, and our society.

To have knowledge is to live better, to have more pleasure, new perspectives, and more discoveries. Knowledge helps us bear our burdens of uncertainty. On the other hand, new knowledge leads to new uncertainties.

This book reveals many discoveries and shares many reflections. The knowledge provided is instructive, motivational, and delightful to read, all at the same time. Ricardo Betti does not limit himself merely to showing the paths to success in the process of admission to the major business schools in the United States. He also enriches us with his stories, his passion for what he does, and his defense of both freedom of choice and the right to happiness through study and work.

Ricardo Betti helps people achieve their dreams. Nobler still, the dreams of others become his from the first handshake.

Although he presents schools and candidates as the main characters in this book, allow me to tell you the truth from the start: the real protagonist is Ricardo Betti, the author, through his just and true labor. He is a sensitive, profound person with ethical principles; he is courageous and contemporary, intellectual, and warm-hearted, a true philosopher in search of truth in reason and feelings.

To write a foreword to a book is to support it. When one accepts this honor and responsibility, one is validating and endorsing the work. He who gives approval shares responsibility for the book. I am not going to run away from this responsibility. This is a unique book, written by a special author, full of lessons for those who want to complete a master's in business administration, those who have already received one, the parents of students who want to get an MBA, or simply for those who like good stories with happy endings—true stories of winners, people who sought to reach their dreams and did so with the help of someone who knows how to dream and make the dreams of others come true, someone who stands solidly alongside his clients throughout their journeys.

I receive many requests to write forewords and refuse most of them because I do not feel I can recommend a book without knowing its content and its author well. It would not be fair to the reader. It would take a lot of time to read all the books that I am asked to read—it would greatly increase my stress level. No stress arose, however, from reading this book. On the contrary, I read it twice with great pleasure.

Following the style of the author himself, I resorted to the Dicionário Houaiss da Língua Portuguesa (the *Antonio Houaiss Dictionary of the Portuguese Language),* which defines foreword as "to announce in advance, precede, herald." So I want to announce in advance that this will be a reference work, because it demystifies the process of selection at the major business schools in the world and shows the importance of having a clear strategy to pursue the goal of being admitted at one of these institutions. Above all, I can announce the benefit of this book to the reader who dreams of great things.

This is not a guidebook to the MBA degree. This book is much more than that. It tells the stories of people's dreams and realities and recounts their achievements. It contains lessons about having discipline, focus, and organization, as well as examples of combining a positive attitude with a good strategy. In the end, it allows us to know a very special person, Ricardo Betti, who was first a doctor, but ended up discovering a different calling—not to save lives, but to awaken souls.

More important than just surviving is living in the fullness of knowing you have achieved your dreams. Sometimes people end up wasting their lives with the wrong career, with badly chosen goals that lead to a lack of recognition or the absence of the feeling of victory, of connection with others, of spiritual and professional growth.

Here, reader, you will find information, knowledge and, more than that, inspiration for a new kind of life.

The philosopher Democritus, in his circa 400 BC book *On the Disposition of the Wise Man,* suggests that happiness lies in idleness: "Occupy your mind with little in order to be happy," he instructs. Ricardo Betti replies in turn, without any intent of confrontation,

"Occupy your mind with a lot of what gives you pleasure in order to be happy."

Thank you, Ricardo, for the lessons you teach here, and for sharing with us your fantastic experiences that define you as the "the person who makes dreams come true."

—Carlos Alberto Júlio
Renowned business professor, lecturer, entrepreneur,
and best-selling author of many books,
including the *Economics of Cedar*

Preface

It was a Sunday morning in São Paulo. I was meeting my old friend Paulo for coffee and a chat. The year was 1983. We were old friends who knew each other well, having attended the same elementary, middle, and high schools, and then medical school. We met for a conversation about a subject that was making me lose sleep at night. At the time, I was splitting my days between the medical clinic of a large Brazilian bank called Banco Itaú and a hospital where I assisted in vascular surgeries. Paulo, older than me by eleven months, was already established in his career as a pathologist. He was anxious to know what was on my mind that Sunday morning. I did not leave him in suspense long.

After we had been served our coffee I announced, "I have decided to leave the medical profession. I want to get an MBA abroad."

"You mean, just like that?" Paulo asked, raising his eyebrows. "What about your career as a doctor at the bank? What about your patients at the clinic? What about the vascular surgery group?" Paulo scratched his head as more questions started flooding to his mind. "And why abroad? Why not here in São Paulo, where all your friends and family live?" He was incredulous.

I rushed to explain, "I don't want to be a physician anymore; I'm tired of it. As you well know, medicine has never been quite my thing. I want to study business administration. I want to travel and see the world, meet people from other areas. Besides, Banco Itaú has agreed to sponsor me—as long as I get into a top-ten program in the US and commit to working at the bank for at least two years afterward, no longer in the medical field, but in human resources instead. Doing the MBA abroad is a great chance to learn how other cultures do business and to network with people from all around the world. That way I will have the possibility of working in other countries, opening new windows of opportunity for me. As for the clinic, I'll transfer my patients to Dr. Alvaro; I'm sure he will not complain about it." I took a deep breath. It felt good to put into words the thoughts that had been weighing me down for so long. Already I felt lighter.

Paulo, however, seemed to feel heavier. It was his turn to sigh. The burden had been transferred to him, at least until he could be sure his old friend hadn't lost his mind. He asked, "But what does it take to get into a program like that? What schools are we talking about?"

"Well, in a nutshell, I'll have to do some exams—basically the TOEFL (Test of English as a Foreign Language) and the GMAT (Graduate Management Admission Test)—send in my college transcript, write a few essays in English on topics defined by the universities, attach two letters of recommendation from people I've worked with, and send a one-page résumé. The schools I'm looking at are MIT, Stanford, Harvard, Wharton, Kellogg, Columbia, Chicago, Michigan, Tuck, and Berkeley."

Paulo scratched his head and absentmindedly looked out the window at the Sunday morning passersby. He said, "It seems like a lot of work, especially the essays. What kind of topics are they usually about?"

"Some are fairly obvious; for example, 'What are your career goals?'; 'Why do you want an MBA?'; 'What are your greatest achievements/ professional accomplishments?'; 'Why did you choose this school?' and so on. Others, however, are more elaborate; for example, 'Describe an ethical dilemma you faced and explain how you solved it,' and 'Mention a teamwork situation in which your objectives weren't achieved,' or 'Comment on one occasion in which you defended a point contrary to the view of the majority,' and some other topics that are just as terrifying. In general, the size of these essays varies from three hundred to a thousand words, depending on the school."

"I can see you've put some research time into this. Do you know what you're going to write?"

"That's where I want to count on your help. Considering that two heads are better than one, I'd like to discuss the contents with you before writing the essays. The annoying part is that we have to do it on Sunday mornings, since we're busy every other day."

"You know you can count on me, buddy," Paulo said. "As a matter of fact, I think it'll be fun to help you sell yourself."

Throughout the process, we did everything we could think of to produce the very best essays possible, designed to impress the admissions officers at the desired schools. The result was terrific: I was admitted to all of them except Harvard. I opted for MIT, where I had a terrific academic, personal, and professional experience. Nonetheless, I never forgot those brainstorming sessions—those Sunday insights were critical to my success and ended up serving as an inspiration for a new career, which finally fully satisfied my professional aspirations. I never imagined that I would become an educational consultant specializing in helping people sell themselves to get into the best MBA courses in the world. But here I am.

I consider myself fortunate to have built a truly innovative career focused on human development. And that's precisely what this book is about—human development—a practical approach, based on real cases, aiming to inspire readers to take charge of their lives and build a successful future, consistent with their aspirations and potential. Originally meant for Brazilian readers, it has been translated into English so that readers around the world can delight in its lessons while learning about Brazilian culture and some of the business leaders who have helped Brazil finally find its place in the sun.

Acknowledgments

I am indebted to my wife, Sandra Betti, my tireless supporter, one of the three founding partners of our São Paulo–based HR consulting company (*MBA Empresarial*), and really the main pillar of the company. Without her support, none of this would have happened—from the time of working on my MBA at MIT, when she faced the burden of managing the house and raising kids while I devoted myself to books (and she still managed to complete her master's studies at Harvard)—up to today, when her commitment, energy, and infinite wisdom light the way for our customers and employees. The word *love* is not enough to express what I feel for her, my better half since the age of fifteen. The feedback I received from Sandra as I wrote this book always put it back on the right track.

I would also like to thank our business partner, Satiko Monobe. She has been present in all the most important moments of our company and is permanently dedicated to collaborating with my educational consulting work, especially in the recruitment processes of companies that sponsor employees for MBA programs (Banco Itaú-Unibanco, Gerdau, RBS, and Santander in Brazil). She is constantly updating our knowledge about rankings and bringing to our attention articles in the international press about MBA programs.

Likewise, in the last eleven years, I have had the dedicated support of our secretary, Leticia Barile, a true *fac totum* who, among myriad other things, manages my complicated schedule and captivates my clients with her friendliness and efficiency, celebrating every admission.

The task of collecting my memories and transforming them into organized and coherent texts was greatly facilitated by the involvement of another very special person who I am proud to have had as a partner throughout this project: Ricardo Ramos Filho, better known as Caco. The grandson of the great Brazilian author Graciliano Ramos and son of Ricardo Ramos, he is a childhood friend who was born with a writer's pedigree. From school age forward, he demonstrated great skill in writing, an activity that he now combines with a corporate career in the field of information technology.

Author of such books and e-books as *Sentimental Computer, Dream Among Friends, The Little Grain of Sand, Noah's Boat, João Bolão, The Book in a Shell, In the Macaroni's Plate, Olivia, The Book Without Pictures*, and *One, Two, Three, Each One On His Turn*, among others, this friend who signs his books as Ricardo Filho had the patience to hear my stories and revise my writing, making it more literary and less dry, in order to reach a final product that we are both immensely proud of. Thank you, Caco.

I am also grateful to Carlos Alberto Julio, himself an accomplished writer, communicator, entrepreneur, lecturer, and business consultant, someone whom I admire very much. He honored me by writing the foreword to this book.

Mayra Monobe, our graphic designer, who now lives in Spain, also lent her talent to develop the cover of the book, which relates the central theme of the work to the place where the final stage of development took place—sunny Lucca, in Tuscany. Thanks to Mayra for the great work.

Vanessa Blatt Rossi was the person in charge of translating the book into English, conducting also the task of interacting with the publisher. Her competent and diligent work was paramount to materializing the English version.

Another great friend who read the first draft in English and motivated me to go ahead with the project was Maxx Duffy, in my opinion the wisest admissions consultant on planet Earth. Her husband, John Vorhaus, an accomplished writer, editor, and international creative consultant, did an excellent editing job, making my text more palatable to American readers. Thank you both.

I could not launch my first book without thanking my parents, Danilo and Laura, for their love and their arduous battle to ensure I received a good education. From them, I received the best inheritance—nonquantifiable but clearly present in all my actions—an unquenchable sense of love and compassion for others.

Finally, I wish to honor my son and my daughter, Mauricio and Renata, to whom I have tried to convey everything I've learned from my clients. Both were excellent students and have prepared themselves in the best possible way for a globalized marketplace. They already know English far better than I did at their ages, have done several courses abroad, and worked in leading companies, building successful careers that are compatible with their profiles, without the worry of starting all over, like me, in search of professional achievement.

I consider myself privileged to have this family who supports me and applauds me in good times and bad, always seeking to grow and to help others—without which, life would be pointless. It was in this spirit that we wrote this book and hope it will be a source of encouragement and reflection for new possibilities.

Ricardo Betti

Introduction

I have been working as an educational consultant for twenty-four years. During this period, I've helped many people achieve their goal of attaining an international MBA. As of January 2011, I've counseled 1,212 clients, and together they've had 2,610 admissions. My alma mater, MIT Sloan, admitted 161 of my clients; the University of Michigan (Ross) admitted 152; the University of Chicago (Booth), 129; the University of Pennsylvania (Wharton), 127; London Business School,121; Columbia, 116; and NYU (Stern) and Northwestern (Kellogg) admitted more than 100 combined. The two most selective schools—Stanford and Harvard—admitted 58 and 50, respectively. Through the years, my firm has also assisted people interested in undergraduate transfers and other degree programs—the LLM, MSc, MPP, and PhD—bringing our statistics to more than fifteen hundred clients served and over three thousand offers of admission received.

Numbers aside, my greatest reward in this quarter century has been the privilege of spending time with so many intelligent, extraordinary people, all of them so admirably determined to grow intellectually, professionally, and emotionally. They are people from many different origins and backgrounds, from different social groups, ethnicities, and professional experiences, all with the common goal of improving their education within the context of a globalized world.

From my clients, I have learned almost everything I hold true; my inspiration and motivation comes from them, and it is to them that I dedicate this book. I would love to tell my readers the story of every single client, but the impossibility of this task has forced me to select the most representative and unique cases. In the end, I chose only a few dozen people whose life stories cover a wide range of examples that will surely meet the interests of many different audiences.

The people mentioned in this book have all been contacted for permission to share their stories, and they have all answered a questionnaire that was used to validate the information I had and to update me about their career paths after completing their MBAs.

Despite the care to rescue the essential facts, there was also great care to tell these stories *ad libitum,* that is, as they were recorded in my memory, which admittedly may have resulted in romanticized versions that time undertook to crystallize.

To the inaccuracies of memory add the various job switches that our research was not always able to follow. The dynamic nature of careers in business and the accelerated nature of the professional development of holders of MBA degrees make some of these stories already outdated at the time of publication; this fact, however, is not relevant in the context of the book, which seeks mainly to convey the specific time of admission to the MBA and the trajectories of the protagonists prior to embarking on their MBAs.

The attentive reader will notice that, in most chapters, I refer to clients only by first names. Occasionally, I use the initial of their last names to differentiate clients who share the same first name. This is to preserve their privacy. However, I only avoided quoting the companies our clients worked for when the information revealed was confidential.

Thus, the book's organization is based on these reports, interspersed with my comments and analysis—which is aimed at explaining the critical success factors in each case—regarding either admission to an MBA program or career development post-MBA.

—Ricardo Betti 2011

Is it worth it? Everything is worth it if the soul is not small.
—Fernando Pessoa, Portuguese poet

1

Selling Sushi

Whenever a new client comes into my office and I try to explain exactly what my job is as an educational consultant, I realize that it is easy to understand the informative part—choosing the courses most appropriate to each candidate (profile matching), verifying English and mathematical proficiency, referring them to teachers specialized in the TOEFL (Test of English as a Foreign Language) and the GMAT (Graduate Management Admission Test), drawing up a schedule, explaining each step of the selection process—but it is not so easy to explain the intangible component of the process, which is the positioning strategy of the candidate for each school desired. This positioning allows for different nuances in the presentation of facts, but should never hurt our basic premise of always telling the truth.

To facilitate understanding, I use the metaphor of a Japanese restaurant. It goes like this: on a busy street, there are two Japanese restaurants quite similar in size, quality, cost, service, and location. However, one of them is always empty and the other always crowded. The empty restaurant has a sign outside that reads, "We sell overpriced dead fish, and we serve it raw, cold, and sliced." The crowded restaurant, in turn, has a color photo out front of sushi being prepared by a smiling sushi chef, with the inscription, "Come and taste our delicious sushi." Both tell the truth, but quite differently, with directly opposite results.

So it is with the selection process for MBA courses. In some schools, there are over ten thousand candidates for 900 to 950 spots—that is, a less than 10 percent admission rate. Many of the candidates have all the desired qualifications—high scores in the TOEFL and GMATs, solid academic records, good work experience, some international experience, favorable letters of recommendation, and so on. What, then, makes the difference for more than 85 percent of applicants who are rejected at each school? My response: many do not know how to sell sushi. The way a candidate positions him or herself in this competition is undoubtedly the decisive factor in the whole process; it is what will determine the success or failure of a whole life plan. In our office—modesty aside—we know how to sell sushi. Here, 92 percent of our customers achieve their goal of getting into a top MBA program.

Truthfully, if any one of our clients were to write an autobiography, they would probably quickly fill a book two hundred pages long or more. They have so many interesting things to share. But in the MBA admissions process, applicants are forced by the required word constraints imposed by each university to limit themselves to a total of five to ten pages. What are the ten most important pages among the potential two hundred of a person's autobiography? Which 5 percent of a person's life should decide 100 percent of his or her future? That is the challenge in positioning yourself. So, yes, telling the truth is important, but the challenge lies in doing so in a way that helps you win the game. Positioning yourself also means differentiating yourself from your competitors.

If you are an engineer or businessperson and work in consulting or the financial market, chances are you'll have hundreds—maybe thousands—of competitors with the exact same profile. What will make the Admissions Office of X School choose one applicant and not another? It is the details one of them offers that will make a difference. It is the paths one of them has traveled, the examples of experiences given, the extracurricular activities the applicant has engaged in. Anything can be important, so long as it is placed in the proper perspective.

When my friend Paulo helped me in my brainstorming sessions, we were not sure whether we should inform the admission officers that I was a backgammon referee. Or that during college I wrote skits for the Med School Follies Show, in addition to playing the piano. It was information that could be omitted without harming the whole, but I decided to use them as examples of versatility and multiplicity of interests which, by intuition, we thought could weigh in my favor.

Today, I *know* these things are important, as are applicants' family backgrounds and their involvement in community activities.

These details, if properly revealed, become what we call hooks, and these hooks are what bring the desired result. To demonstrate their importance, we have used them to organize the structure of this book: each title of almost every chapter names the hook we used to capture an admission officer's attention and arouse interest in our applicant. In the exceptions, the title refers to where professional success led our client post-MBA. Such is the propulsion potential in a good hook.

2

The Gold Watch

Our first interview with a potential MBA applicant is always free. This is how the client and I evaluate whether there is empathy between us, a good fit, and a willingness to work together. Normally it takes ten to twenty-five meetings to produce material for the application, depending on the number of schools to which the person is applying, so compatibility is key.

On this particular Tuesday, I was holding a first interview with a young gentleman by the name of Rodrigo, who had long brown hair and a solid physique. He sat in front of me speaking quite firmly, getting straight to the point. It did not take him long to refer to a hurdle between him and his goal. He had great difficulty with tests and did not know whether the good grades he had obtained in college would be sufficient to gain admission to a prestigious program. He asked me straight out what his chances were, not wanting to waste time. If his chances were almost minimal, as he thought might be the case, he would consider calmly letting go of his desire to accomplish an MBA. What was clearly an old insecurity hidden behind a studied assertiveness was rearing its head. We talked a lot. I made him see by the end of our first meeting that it was worth a shot.

In the next two meetings, we used a technique I always use—brainstorming—to deepen our understanding of the task at hand. Rodrigo told me details of his life, career, successes, joys, disappointments. Free-associating such stories can provide lots of insights. When we are freed from thinking in a logical sequence and allowed to go back and forth in time, seeking anecdotal memories that may even be almost forgotten, people end up revealing that one bit of information that makes all the difference. Brainstorming, then, is a force that opens the door to the dream.

This is where my experience is crucial. I have learned to search carefully for the gold in the story of a client's life and discover what makes him or her special. Mostly, I look for *the* story—that one particular and beautiful moment when my clients reveal the thing they most seek. I was deeply touched by this story that Rodrigo told me and have never forgotten it:

> My father, an airline pilot, died when I was very small. He did not leave me much besides memories. He did, however, leave one material thing, something full of meaning, symbolic if you will. With it, I marked the time from then on. It was a gold watch.
>
> I remember staring at the second hand till I drooped. Watching it turning, turning, feeling entranced, deep in the past. It always made me sad. I kept the watch in the nightstand drawer. Sometimes, when I dreamed of my old man, I woke in the night, lit the lamp, looking for the watch in the drawer, searching for that golden glow I knew so well. Then I would bring it to my ear and listen to the endless whispered ticking. I never forgot to wind it. I did not want to ever see it stopped. The ticking was like a beating heart; a living inheritance from my father.
>
> Time did not bring my father back. Instead, it turned him sepia. He became a shadow in my memory.
>
> At sixteen, I decided I needed an international experience. I needed to travel, see other parts of the world, learn a language other than Portuguese. But I had no money to pay for my dream. Only it was not a dream to me. It was a necessity. I felt that my future would depend on being able to travel at that time in my life, a time when my mother could barely look me in the eyes, so ashamed was she of not being able to help. I feel badly for her even today; I know now how hard it must have been.
>
> I decided to sell the watch. I mean . . . it wasn't like that, from one moment to another. I suffered a lot. I went back

and forth many times before the final step. Even today, I remember the day I sold the watch. I felt lost, bewildered; the money in my pocket seemed to burn my skin underneath it. It was a horrible shame, a feeling of guilt that has never really left me.

The amount I got for the watch was small, but enough for the ticket and some pocket money. Off I went to Europe, without a definite plan. With the amount raised, I could not expect much from the adventure. In France, I got a job as an au pair.

I took care of a boy with severe physical disabilities. I took him to physical therapy every day. I was moved by the boy's struggle and I gave him the best care I could. I felt really great affection for him. And then luck smiled at me. The boy's father, impressed with the devotion that I had in caring for his child, and knowing of my financial troubles, granted me a spot in a course at the university at which he was a dean. I was able to stay there for a significant amount of time. For someone who only had had money for the plane ticket, it had been a victory.

I came back. The time I'd spent abroad was crucial to obtaining employment as a trainee in a multinational company, where my career quickly advanced. That's when I began my university studies in earnest. And the second hand did not take as many turns around the proverbial clock face as I had anticipated in order to accomplish all of this.

I have made many friends at work. Many remain friends still. This is only natural for, with so many intimate details revealed, I end up creating a place in my heart for them, a place filled with trust, respect, and affection. There's always something about their stories with which I identify, and that ultimately brings us together beyond the work we are trying to do. Rodrigo was no exception. I was touched by the challenges he faced, from childhood forward, and from the lack of money in his household. Having also come from a humble family, remembering well the sacrifices that my parents made to give the best possible education to their two children, I have always felt moved by people with financial troubles.

The story of the watch, I'm sure, was decisive for Rodrigo to be admitted to the Thunderbird School of Global Management in Glendale, Arizona, a highly-ranked international business school. When we decided to tell it in his essay, we knew it was full of meaning and strength, a passport to the program he wanted. After that, overcoming his difficulty with the GMAT was a simple matter of training.

Upon completing his MBA at Thunderbird, Rodrigo accepted a job working for one of the largest food companies in the world. Later, having somewhat of an entrepreneurial spirit, he switched to the editorial area, where he is today a very successful executive. He has lived and worked in the United States since 1997.

3

The Self-Made Man

When dealing with people on a close personal basis, it's difficult to remain indifferent to certain characteristics of their personalities. In not-so-straightforward ways, we end up identifying with the difficulties they confront, the paths they choose, and the moods that prevail. With Osvaldo, it was no different. In our first conversation, I saw a lot of myself in him—the same tendency to introversion and the same shyness. I also saw in Osvaldo an iron will to grow and to offset a humble beginning by lifting barriers.

Osvaldo was born in Santos. His family had little formal education. His father was a chauffeur and his mother a housekeeper. Consequently, he had access only to the rather precarious Brazilian public schools. However, through much effort and studying on his own, he got into ITA (Instituto Tecnológico de Aeronáutica), a renowned Brazilian university that trains engineers to build airplanes. Undisputedly one of the best engineering schools in the country and also one of the hardest to get into, it offers free tuition and subsidized housing once admission is gained. Upon entering ITA, Osvaldo took a big step toward the independence he desired and needed. Here is his story, as I remember it, of course:

> I gradually freed myself from the English dictionary. It became less and less often that I had to look up the words I needed to read, to understand, and to use later in my own writing.

Blessed was the moment when I joined the Pen Pal Association. Those solitary exchanges of letters with friends at an unknown distance, letter by letter, word for word, began to bear fruit. Already I could understand, almost without interruption, entire texts written in English. Finally, I was progressing. Now I just needed to broaden my horizons—to write to more people. Quantity would make a difference. The more cards I received, the more I would have to answer. The more letters I answered and the more training I had, the more knowledge and foreign language proficiency I would get.

I yawned. The words danced and mingled under my weary student eyes. *Just a little bit more*, I whispered to myself, pushing, motivating myself to push beyond my limits. I stretched and massaged my sore neck.

Jeff, my friend from San Francisco, had written of a novelty that had begun to appear in the United States: the Internet. "One day we will not write letters anymore," he wrote. "We will receive messages through electronic media, on our computers." I found that inspiring. I could tell that the world was changing quickly—it was shrinking—and this made me even more determined to stay ahead of the curve.

While in college, Osvaldo never had any money. There is a trip to Europe that students take at the end of the course at ITA. It is part of the tradition of the school. Osvaldo couldn't afford to go. He stayed behind, working. He dedicated himself to a temporary job he had gotten at *Infraero*, the government organ responsible for the Brazilian airport infrastructure, coincidentally the first major client of my own HR consulting company, *MBA Empresarial*. We were working together with a group of teachers from his university on the project.

The project's aim was to collect and statistically analyze all the operational variables that impacted the functioning of airports in Rio de Janeiro and São Paulo (more than two thousand variables) in order to set up guidelines for future expansions. My company's job was to recruit, train, and supervise interns responsible for data collection (about eighty people in all, between those in Rio de Janeiro and those in São Paulo).

Osvaldo stood out in the selection process when asked about his work preferences for the Traveler Profile phase of the project. Without hesitation, he chose to interview foreign passengers arriving in Brazil. It was the way he had found to practice spoken English, since he only knew how to communicate in the language through writing. He is one of the few people I know who learned a new language on his own, without a teacher or classes.

After graduating, he began working with the Brazilian bank, Banco Itaú, where he was hired after going through a highly competitive selection process. As always, he dedicated himself wholeheartedly and was rewarded for it. At the end of three years, he won a full scholarship to complete an MBA abroad. Again, coincidentally, there was our firm, *MBA Empresarial*, selecting and preparing candidates. He got a 780 score, out of a possible 800, on the GMAT and was admitted at two of the most difficult programs—Harvard and Stanford. He opted for Stanford. He didn't even want to try the others.

Once he was admitted, he sought me out again. Since he still had half a year before starting the course, he asked me if he could borrow books from my MBA program. He intended to study the material before he started graduate school. I remember watching him leave my office carrying a huge stack of books. On the eve of his departure to Stanford, he gave me back the books, informing me that he had studied everything. Two years of reading in six months! I had never seen anything like it.

After he completed his MBA, he returned to Brazil and to the bank, where he reached the position of director in only two years. He became one of the youngest directors in the history of the bank. By that time, he had overcome his shyness and insecurity. He had grown a lot as a person.

During his time as director—responsible, among other things, for the products area—he helped the bank increase its market share by 5 percent, reaching the highest share in the Brazilian market, which is very fragmented and has many formidable competitors.

Mission accomplished, he left that company to pursue another dream: to open his own construction business. He said he wanted to create the best business of its kind in Brazil. I did not doubt that he would succeed. With a focus on building homes for the upper middle class, his firm has been growing rapidly since he started it. In a short space of time, the company has reached an enviable level, delivering an average of one house per month and giving him a very comfortable standard of living.

Osvaldo is married and has one daughter. Nowadays, he considers his family his main focus and strives to maintain a good balance between his personal and professional life.

When I think of people who came from nothing and made it big, I always think of Osvaldo, although he affirms with great modesty that several people helped him along the path. When I draw a parallel between his story and my own, I encounter the image of my mother. She has always been a guiding force; an inspiration in my life. She is still the teacher who is always there for her students and for me. We all have someone or something on our side. Osvaldo had only the incentive from his poor parents to study—that and an immense sense of willpower. He taught himself to seek inspiration and, in that way, gained his independence step by step.

My job was to identify the beauty in the story of that young man from Santos who overcame so much, and to endow him with confidence. After that, I had only to applaud him. In truth, I did very little for someone who hardly needed me. After all, he was used to getting by on his own.

4

The Midas Touch

Carlos F. is someone who might have helped me more than I helped him. A self-made man, he started his entrepreneurial career early, while still in college. This is how I picture his start:

> It would be a different kind of meeting. It was unusual for students to get together at the engineering school of the University of São Paulo for any reason other than to study. Convening the group with no apparent reason put everyone on the alert. Everyone was curious to hear Carlos F.'s idea.
>
> "We need to start a company," he told them. "It's time to start earning our living."
>
> They liked the idea, and got to work straightaway. It was a simple idea. They formed a package delivery service, a Brazilian version of Federal Express. They went, and they conquered. In a short period of time, they had already rented a hangar. Five years later, when they sold their business at an excellent profit, the five original employees had grown to five hundred employees, plus a considerable fleet. They had become big; they had become leaders in the Brazilian market for the delivery of goods bought online. Carlos F. took his share from the sale and used it to pay his tuition for an MBA program abroad. It was more than enough to cover the cost without having to ask for money from his father, a self-made man who owned a luxury hotel but who believed his children needed to make and spend their own fortunes.

Talking with Carlos F. was always pleasant. Dynamic, charismatic, and enterprising, he inspired those around him. When I later asked him to what he attributed his admission to so many MBA programs, he was blunt:

"Diversity. I made it a point to broaden my horizons. I was a professional keyboardist for over six years; I am a commercial pilot and have been a practitioner of equestrian riding for almost ten years. I like studying languages. I am fluent in Spanish, French, and English."

The secret behind his successful diversity might lie in his diligent organization and forward planning: while still a sophomore at college, Carlos F. had made a detailed chart of the income levels he wanted to achieve over the next twenty years. When he later showed me these estimates, I was shocked by their accuracy. Much of it had already been completed, surprisingly close to what he had planned for himself.

Carlos F. got a 620 the first time he took the GMAT and a 630 the second time. He had a hard time accepting this, since he had been getting over 700 in the practice tests. He was persistent and tried again, getting 700 on his third attempt; it was his style to never give up in the face of obstacles.

In his essays, we explored the multiplicity of his interests and his entrepreneurial spirit. We included his compensation chart as a way of demonstrating his capacity for planning and setting goals. I can't always safely say that someone will be admitted to a specific school, especially a very selective one (at the time only 6 percent of applicants were admitted to Stanford), but I was so confident he would get in that I bet a dinner at his father's hotel on it. If he didn't get in, I'd pay the bill.

To my double delight, I won the bet, and we had dinner in this unique hotel where famous people stayed. The model Naomi Campbell, for example, dined quietly a few feet away from us, with no idea of the reason for so much joy at our table, as we heartily celebrated Carlos F.'s hard-won and much-deserved victory.

The characteristics explored in Carlos F.'s application continued to mark his life after the MBA degree. When he returned to Brazil, he founded a university in the northeastern state of Ceará. In just a few years, it reached an enrollment of three thousand students and was already considered the fourth best university in the state. He is expanding to other states in the region, believing in the huge growth potential of the education sector in northeastern Brazil.

I do not lie when I say that I have learned everything I know from my clients. When I got an offer to sell my own business, I sought out Carlos F. for his advice, even though he is much younger than I am. Despite his youth, he was already seasoned in the business world. Thanks to his considered input, I declined to sell, and my company is still going strong.

5

The Boy Wonder

My impression is that inertia is one of the most powerful forces in nature. It is present in everything. It is easily identified in the realm of physics and widely studied in school. It appears, however, with equal strength, in the emotional arena. We tend to keep going on the same path our whole lives. We are very reluctant to accept deviations. That is why it was so hard for me to leave the medical profession. The process was slow and painful. It took me a while—a time in which I was in constant internal turmoil—to realize that I no longer wanted to pursue that profession. Where had my childhood dreams gone? Without my noticing, those dreams had turned into a nightmare. I violated my true self every day by simply continuing what I had begun, working without taking pleasure in it.

Many people in seemingly hopeless situations lose heart and settle for less than is possible, opting unconsciously for unhappiness. Then they spend their lives like a robot, sad from lacking the joy of doing what they love. Although there are no statistics, I'm sure these robots correspond to the majority of people. It is rare to find someone who is passionate about what he or she does. Often work is seen as a burden, a heavy fate that has been reserved for us.

Hoping to inject a different view of the future in young people, my wife spurred us to implement a nonprofit project of vocational guidance for seventy teenagers. We called the program MBA Teens. We knew very well how difficult it can be for a young person to choose his or her future appropriately. How can someone choose if he or she doesn't have enough information? At the time, the common thing was for people to use vocational tests, questionnaires, and interviews to decide on their future careers. This approach was full of questions and answers allegedly capable of helping them make up their minds. For us, with our own children approaching college age, this approach seemed inadequate. We envisioned a continued and progressive process, aimed at developing the emotional intelligence of young people. Through games, simulations, lectures by professionals from various fields, interviews, and other activities, we could provide more favorable conditions for this huge decision.

To make the project possible, we rented a property and invested considerable capital in its renovation and adaptation, working around the clock to balance these activities with our many other day-to-day responsibilities. Unfortunately, the project grew beyond our financial capabilities at the time, and we were not able to continue with it.

I still consider this project one of the best I've ever participated in. We've kept track of many of the seventy teenagers, and have derived great satisfaction from seeing them become successful in various professions. In the group, there are administrators, consultants, marketing and communications specialists, engineers, psychologists, a journalist, an architect, an international model, and an airline pilot.

One day, we received a call from a young man, Cláudio, who was interested in the project. He had set up an NGO in Brazil and was affiliated with another international NGO, both of them in education. He came from a family of Japanese immigrants who, like thousands of others from Japan, had built new lives for themselves in Brazil. He volunteered to join our NGO. We soon learned that he had graduated as an architect but did not intend to work in that area; one more person who had noticed early on that he needed to rethink his chosen field of study.

He made a great impression on us, and we asked if he would be interested in being a trainee at our human resources company. Although he had no experience in HR, it was clear that he had great potential. His life story was full of accomplishments: He had gotten first place in one of the most difficult college admission exams in Brazil. He had been a local tennis champion and had even represented Brazil in other countries in the sport. In short, he excelled at everything he set out to do.

We were right to bet on him. Cláudio picked up the work so fast that soon he began to participate in the company's other projects, including the international ones. When we first met him, his only foreign language was intermediate English. I lent him a Spanish course on CD-ROM, which had been languishing in my drawer for about three years without ever having been opened. Swiftly, and through self-education, he became fluent enough in the language to make presentations to executives in Mexico, Peru, and Colombia. Remarkably, in one month, he achieved the status of senior consultant in our company. He had learned in that time what people normally take two years to learn.

Next, he became interested in getting his MBA and very quickly scored an impressive 750 on the GMAT. In the meantime, he was working toward a certificate in business administration at a competitive Brazilian university, obtaining very high grades as he prepared for the courses he would encounter in any MBA program.

He did brainstorming sessions with me to figure out what to write in his essays. He still was not clear about what career he would like to embrace in the future but felt certain that he wanted to do something related to nonprofit work.

Cláudio did very well in the admissions process and was admitted at various schools with scholarships. The schools soon started fighting over him, offering him higher and higher scholarships. In the end, he decided to go to Stanford, accepting their rare offer of a full scholarship.

Upon completing his MBA, Cláudio went to Japan to study his Japanese origins. He located relatives who had never heard of him, an initiative that served to unite his family after two generations of separation. His Japanese relations were so moved and delighted by him that they ended up coming to his wedding in São Paulo.

After his graduation, he still wanted to work in the nonprofit sector, but then received an attractive proposal to work in an investment bank in New York, something that contrasted sharply with his original goals. He would be moving from nonprofit work to the most intense form of capitalism, with no stops along the way. It was another difficult decision for him, but Cláudio had learned to be unafraid of unknown paths. He accepted the bank's proposal; however, he continued to do nonprofit work in his spare time. In just a few years, his life had taken several twists: he had gone from being an architect, tennis player, and volunteer worker to being an HR consultant and then a finance professional. From boy wonder to high-powered executive—just another example of what can be achieved when you set old dreams aside and focus on new goals.

6

Far from Home

Getting an MBA abroad was a unique experience for me, a turning point in my career, and a transformation for my life. At MIT, I met an extremely intelligent group of people with the most diverse professional and cultural backgrounds imaginable. From the Cameroonian Moyo, educated at the Sorbonne and able to sing bossa nova in perfect Portuguese (even though he could not speak the language) to the Australian lawyer Simon, owner of a mattress factory; the unforgettable figure of Asad, a polo champion from Singapore; Luc, the Belgian who was fluent in six languages; the French Alain, who had won several awards in financial accounting; the Lebanese Paul, an investment genius; the Spaniard Rafael, a friend of King Juan Carlos and the owner of a railroad in his homeland; the Portuguese Jose, an ace in conflict management; and many other amazing colleagues from various countries whose stories could fill another book.

Among my American classmates, I well remember Jack, a doctor like me, who would become chief of the medical department at MIT; John, an excellent cook who gave memorable parties—one with the theme of Do It Yourself, where he spent the night teaching his guests to make sophisticated Japanese dishes; Lynn, an accomplished professional who sought to supplement her PhD in nutrition with an MBA; Michael, who claimed the advantage of having studied for the GMAT while working as a night watchman; Richard, an insurance salesman from Missouri who spoke like a TV announcer; Beth, an artist; Elizabeth, a professional comedian; Robin, who created Zipcar (rental cars by the hour) during the MBA and later became very wealthy from it; and Steve, a literature professor who recited Shakespeare during breaks between classes.

There were few Brazilians at MIT back then, in 1984. In my class, it was just me and Ulysses, an engineer who helped me master the quantitative material from the program. Outside of the MBA program, there were enough Brazilians at MIT, mostly in engineering, to warrant our having a small room we proudly named the Brazilian Club, where we avidly read out-of-date Brazilian magazines sent to us by slow post from home.

We Brazilians ended up making friends with the Latin Americans (especially the Argentines) and many Europeans, but rarely with the Americans, who were often more focused on their academic performance than their social lives.

The MBA grading system is usually based on comparative grades (forced distribution of grades based on the bell curve), a factor that stimulates competition since the success of a student depends on the failure of others. American students take this system very seriously. At MIT, some colleagues kept their competitive advantage over foreigners like me, who still had difficulty understanding some of the things the professor said, by covering their notes with their hands so that others could not see what they had written—something that would be unthinkable in Brazil.

The workload was overwhelming, and every teacher acted like he or she was the only one, assigning tons of homework. From the first day of classes, I had to deal with a pace of work I had never faced before—even in the most difficult times during my internship in the emergency room. *If I survived the ER*, I used to think, *I can survive anything.* I had been fooling myself. So great was the burden, that in the first semester I thought about quitting, something that is not in my nature. The economics classes, for example, required knowledge that I did not have, forcing me to attend remedial classes on Saturdays, and thus stealing from other subjects precious hours of study. The engineers had an easy time with those courses, but at least I got my revenge in organizational behavior and marketing courses, where the ability to write was more important than the ability to do complicated calculations.

In the second year, when I could take electives, the situation improved greatly, for I developed a skill that I baptized "selective neglect." I learned to prioritize and manage my time better in order to fulfill almost all obligations, leaving out only the least important.

In the midst of this marathon of studies, my classmates and I found time to party. I remember that at one of the parties I was a big hit dressed as Professor Bitran, a Brazilian who had a brilliant career at MIT and was the head of the operations department. I bought glasses with a fake nose and mustache, and my colleagues swore that I looked just like him. Coincidentally, he ended up being my thesis adviser the following year, and I came to admire him greatly for his vast knowledge and impressive quantitative skills.

We students also managed to travel, despite our limited financial resources. We went to Canada twice, New York several times, Newport twice, to Washington, DC, and the West Coast cities of Los Angeles, San Francisco, and Las Vegas. There were also short trips to Maine, Vermont, and the coast of Massachusetts: Cape Cod's Provincetown, Plymouth on the North Shore, and other towns, including Gloucester, the fisherman's village where *The Perfect Storm* was filmed.

We had a lot of group projects, but the teaching methods were very well balanced—50 percent case studies and 50 percent lectures—which made the coursework quite varied. In addition to regular classes, we had talks with celebrities from the business world, including Akio Morita and John Reed, both stars of the business world at that time. Also interesting were the company presentations, which aimed to attract new talents to corporate careers.

Between the first and second years, we MBA students took summer jobs, which over the years have become more involving and demanding, and almost compulsory in the perception of most students. The summer job is an opportunity to engage in temporary work at a large company (very well paid, I might add, in the range of US$5,000 to US$8,000 per month), where both sides—student and company—get the opportunity to meet and assess whether there is a match to justify hiring the student after the MBA.

In my case, as I was sponsored by my employer, I returned to Brazil in the summer and worked in the human resources area at Banco Itaú. Today, and with hindsight, I believe that I should have tried to obtain their permission to do my summer job at another company, perhaps in Europe, in order to maximize my exposure to other business realities, but at the time, I didn't think of it.

In Brazil in the eighties, nobody knew what a summer job was, and even today most companies are surprised to learn that in other countries, people pay well to hire employees for only three months. Indeed, it is a fierce competition among the companies offering summer jobs, as they seek to hire the best MBA students from the top schools, which explains the inflated salaries.

Throughout my MBA period, I received a lot of encouragement to engage in networking and to consolidate friendships outside the classroom, a skill that has generated lifelong benefits for me. Years later, I visited classmates in Australia, Singapore, and the United States, seeing for myself the impact that networking has in the globalized world of business. In Singapore, for example, I met up with Asad, the former national polo champion and owner of the duty-free stores in Singapore's international airport. He received me with great hospitality, helping me to better understand the culture of that extraordinary country.

Nowadays, I am the president of the MIT Sloan Alumni Club of Brazil, an association that promotes interaction among former MIT students and organizes conferences, dinners, and other events for the MIT community living in Brazil (approximately 260 people). Like MIT, other large schools have alumni clubs in Brazil and in other countries, encouraging alumni to interact, thus enhancing the strength of their networks.

The lessons I learned during the MBA course were vitally important, especially because I was coming from a completely different field, medicine. Nowadays, as a partner in a human resources consulting firm, I use many of the concepts I learned in the MBA program. That said, I usually tell my clients that the whole mass of information they will receive during the course is the lesser benefit of the experience. Information nowadays can be obtained anywhere in the world by anyone with Internet access. But what really justifies the US$160,000 investment in this international adventure are the intangibles—life experience, cultural exposure, networking, friendship, maturity, and fluency in the vocabulary of business, not to mention the weight of an important brand to put on the résumé. An MBA degree will open doors that would otherwise be closed and provide MBA graduates with an edge over the competition.

7

The Predestined

One of the most extraordinary success stories in my experience is that of Rudi, a participant in the first group of people I coached after I returned from graduate school. We ended up forming a wonderful friendship that has continued through the years. Rudi's career is a remarkable example of the powerful combination of talent and opportunity.

Coincidentally, Rudi and I have many things in common. We went to the same primary and secondary school; we learned Portuguese from the same teacher (the unforgettable Teresa Pujó); we went to the same university (although I studied medicine and he engineering); we were both sponsored by the same bank (Banco Itaú) to get our MBAs; we both went to MIT; and we are both active officers of the MIT Sloan Alumni Club in Brazil. We are also both married to psychologists and each have two children.

Another thing Rudi and I have in common is music. Soon after we met, we started talking about it—the beauty of certain vocal arrangements that can enrapture the listener, the sound of blended voices harmoniously enriching a particular melody . . .

"Have you ever noticed," Rudi commented, "how we are, to some extent, ourselves musical instruments?" Thus a conversation started that led to an invitation to a party at Rudi's house back when he was my client working on his applications with me.

I remember it took me a while to find the address in the neighborhood of Pinheiros, in São Paulo. I was looking for Pedroso de Moraes Street. I finally arrived at a beautiful house located on a well-lit, tree-lined road.

From within came the sound of people singing a familiar bossa-nova tune.

I was met with warmth by the hosts and, within minutes, had made new friends. It was a lively atmosphere, with good food and drinks of the highest quality. Rudi introduced me to the people in the a cappella group performing that night. The music they made with their voices was amazing. I spent an unforgettable night listening to them sing, enthralled, as they sang in perfect pitch, without the need for instruments. No percussion, guitar, piano, or flute; it was only people singing and making sounds normally made with instruments. One person in particular stood out. His name was Paulo Moura. Later, he started a solo career as a musician and became quite famous in Brazil. Success obviously surrounded Rudi.

If I remember correctly, he was admitted to seven or eight of the top schools and was inclined to attend Wharton—though, through my influence, he ended up going to MIT instead.

I know he enjoyed the experience and took advantage of his time abroad. He traveled extensively throughout the world, visiting many countries and expanding his cultural background. The most striking aspect of Rudi's story was, however, his meteoric rise in his post-MBA career. Thanks to his exemplary performance in the international area, and later in the financial area, he received successive promotions and became the youngest chief executive and youngest vice president in the history of Banco Itaú.

The promotions occurred because every time opportunities arose to fill executive positions, whether to replace old leaders or to create new areas, there was Rudi with his obvious talent, knowledge, and willingness to face new challenges.

It is worth mentioning one of my favorite analogies, in which I compare the evolution of careers to sailing on the high seas. The sailor cannot see the shore on the horizon, but he or she knows he must keep the sail taut and in perfect condition, because that way, once the wind comes, he or she will be ready to reach his or hers destination. Rudi is one of those guys who always kept his sails taut, and so was able to take advantage of all the winds that blew in his favor.

Nowadays, he is responsible for the treasury and the financial markets of the bank, managing no less than the bank's cash flow, its market risk, liquidity, financial products, and the relationship with the Central Bank of Brazil. Moreover, he occupies positions on the boards of several companies in the bank's group and of entities in the financial market. I'm sure the money invested by the bank in his MBA has been returned over the years as profit with many zeros added to the end of it.

8

Never Too Late

There once was a boy named Octavio, whose father owned one of the most famous architectural firms in São Paulo. He was the firstborn son and had been raised by his mother. His father had married several times after divorcing Octavio's mother and had many other children, but Octavio was the only one who worked with his father.

Octavio had worked at his father's company since he first started attending a fine arts college. He had never taken his studies very seriously and, working in the family business, had had few opportunities to grow professionally. Although he had been there for ten years when I met him, he was still being given the smallest projects and the easiest ones, work that was not at all stimulating. His curriculum vitae was long but not impressive; there was nothing he felt very proud about, and he was all too lacking in real achievements. In constant conflict with his father, who did not value him, he saw the days go by slowly, feeling little passion for what he did.

I met him the day the responsibility for the renovation of my apartment befell him. We got to talking. I told him what I did, and he became interested in the idea of getting an MBA abroad. I advised him to first take a business specialization course in São Paulo and to improve his English. For the first time in his life, he felt motivated to study. He took my advice and, even now, I can easily imagine him in class . . .

The day had been very hot, and night fell without the temperature dropping. It was getting dark by the time

Octavio got to school. He entered the classroom feeling a pulsing heat that the ceiling fans could not dispel. As he awaited the arrival of the professor, he was lulled by the noise of the blades spinning monotonously. He followed the flight of a moth beating itself against the brilliance of one of the lamps, oblivious to the danger of burns and imminent death . . . so crazy and irresponsible, letting itself become enchanted by the beauty of light. As he watched the frenetic dancing, his eyelids started to feel heavy. For a second, he fell asleep.

"Good evening!"

Octavio opened his eyes, his body and mind immediately snapping to attention, and responded mechanically, "Good evening."

He immediately liked the professor, who dived enthusiastically into the topic of that day's class. He felt himself becoming absorbed by the master's passionate teaching. His reasoning accelerated. He saw how ideas formed by joining thoughts could create a single logical whole. He was learning! He observed the moth again. It was still there—insistent in its plight—but its physical resistance was starting to break down. It was getting weaker. He felt that he could relate. He would have to leave aside his fear, ignore the time he had lost, not worry about the difficulties he would encounter . . . simply allow himself to become enchanted, in a crazy and irresponsible manner, with the beauty of knowledge.

When he finished his training in Brazil, Octavio decided to try for an MBA abroad. He then went through a difficult period in his life. His father, unhappy with his son's new obsession, fired him from the architecture company. At the same time, his mother, his biggest source of affection, died of leukemia. It was with the money she left him that he was able to get by.

He was no longer the same as he had been, still a boy in many ways, weakened by the whims of his father. He was now a man with clear objectives, a strong will, and determination. He was close to thirty years old when he finally blossomed intellectually.

Octavio, thanks to his involvement with architectural projects, had an appreciation for things relating to environmental integration. Nature was his inspiration. He also liked off-road sports. His life's ambition was to design a park.

He studied hard, dedicating himself so much that he was admitted to Yale, one of the most venerable universities in the world. His three-year course would yield master's degrees in both forestry administration and business.

Out of the MBA program, he worked in the largest real-estate company in the world, but Octavio found his ultimate calling in managing an investment fund linked to real estate. Besides the career change, he is now the proud holder of two master's degrees from Yale, and is living proof that it is never too late to chase one's dream.

9

The Brazilian Rock Star

Before I met him, Pedro, today a highly successful professional, used to frequently recall in his dreams his early career as a musician:

There was a lot of excitement backstage. The air was full of a familiar energy that could not be explained. It was a companionable energy: appreciation. It was always like that. Tangible and always present in the minutes before going on stage, it was a wonderful feeling. It was time for the final tuning of the instrument, the final fixing of the hair, the final look in the mirror, the final sip of water. His nerves were as tense as the strings on his bass guitar, full of expectation.

When he finally walked out in front of the audience, he began to relax. There was applause, screaming; the crowd was hungry to hear his music. He happily strummed the bass, gradually building into a frenzied trance, his eyes closed. He played in tune with the drums, giving body to the heavy rhythm. It was magic: chords creating arcs in the air, colored lights flashing, hands clapping wildly. He sang backup vocals, and the crowd shouted the chorus along with him. A huge rush of adrenaline; it was all about the music.

Pedro would awake from that dream with a heavy soul. He had long ago turned away from what was now real only in his dreams. He missed the stage. He missed his old band. He thought of them as an excellent team. The result of the teamwork had been evident in every show. Each band member had a responsibility, a role to fulfill.

Pedro had started playing at an early age in his brother's band. He was a good bassist. As a professional musician, he had traveled all over Brazil, playing to large crowds and experiencing fame. The band's album went platinum and they became well known, especially among young people. Success, however, is not always a constant in the life of an artist. One day, he realized he no longer liked playing in the band so much. They were performing fewer concerts, spending a lot of time being idle, earning less income. Less money, fewer prospects . . . it looked like time for a change.

He had dropped out of an engineering course at Mackenzie University in São Paulo in order to play in the band. Now he decided to go back to school. Upon graduation, he got an internship at ABB, a multinational company that dealt in heavy machinery. He was very successful and was invited to spend six months at company headquarters in Scandinavia as part of a trainee program. There he began to transform himself. He took off his earring and started hiding his tattoos. When he returned to Brazil at the end of the training course, he had already decided to seek an MBA. It was then that he got in touch with me.

During the usual interviews, we noticed some obstacles. His grades in the engineering course were not brilliant—they had only been sufficient to get by and graduate. His English was merely conversational, his grammar far from perfect. It became evident that he would have a hard time getting into a good school.

To improve his chances, we decided to create a strategy based on the duality of his personality. Pedro was very special. He was able to be a rock star or an executive—two completely different things—with the same ease. It was a terrific sign of flexibility. All the details in his life story demonstrated a great versatility as we explored his difficult decision to leave music behind to become an executive. He often talked about how he missed the stage and the exciting atmosphere of concerts.

Pedro's objective was to get into the Kellogg School of Business, the best program for this former rocker's main area of interest, marketing. In truth, this program is always rated near the top in *Business Week*'s ranking of all MBA courses, so attaining admission would be no easy task.

There was also the matter of the interview. It was Pedro's idea to showcase his two personalities to the interviewer, contrasting the rock star with the executive. It is worth noting here the important role of these interviews. At the time of the interview, the candidate is still one among many. What he or she says and does in those few minutes will have to be memorable enough to move and impress the interviewer, for the interview is instrumental in a candidate's admission or rejection. It is an opportunity that cannot be ignored.

Among the options he was given, we decided that Pedro should interview on Kellogg's campus in Evanston, Illinois, near Chicago. He presented himself in a business suit and colorful psychedelic socks that the interviewer would only see when Pedro strategically crossed his legs during the interview. He started the interview talking about his experience as an executive: technical facts, problems, trends, predictions, opinions, all very serious stuff. At a certain point, he began to tell the story of when he was a rocker. That is when he crossed his legs, showing his socks in loud, fun colors, symbolizing his other, more rebellious side. With this move, he certainly hooked the attention of the interviewer. Shortly thereafter, he got an offer of admission.

On his first day of class at Kellogg, Pedro was introduced to the hundreds of students in his class as "the Brazilian Rock Star." They brought him a guitar and asked him to pay homage to a classmate who was celebrating her birthday. He did not make them beg.

Once he finished his MBA, he returned to Brazil to work two jobs: at AB-InBev (AmBev at the time) during the day as the marketing manager of Skol, a well-known brand of beer, and at Mackenzie University in the evenings as a marketing professor.

The work at AB-InBev involved, among other things, attending events sponsored by Skol throughout Brazil. One day's travel by corporate jet would take him from the beaches of Santa Catarina (southern Brazil), to nighttime in Porto de Galinhas, near Recife in Pernambuco (northeastern Brazil), with the full moon illuminating the sea and over a thousand people on the beach dancing and drinking Skol.

As a professor at Mackenzie, he would tell his students, "Teaching is like playing in a rock band—the only difference is that here the music is marketing." At Mackenzie he fell in love with a student who later became his wife.

At the height of his corporate career, Pedro received an offer from Population Services International, a leading global health organization. Accepting it meant moving to Angola and using what he had learned at Kellogg to save the lives of thousands of people by launching products and marketing campaigns for the prevention and treatment of AIDS and malaria, and for promoting contraceptive use, vitamins, food supplements for children, and water treatment. He accepted the job.

Later, that same company transferred him to Washington, DC, where he is now responsible for developing new products in over sixty countries. One day, he'll be off to Laos to launch a new product there, and the next he'll be on Capitol Hill, encouraging US senators to support treatment for childhood pneumonia in developing countries.

I note with satisfaction that the same versatility we used to describe him in his essays continues to drive his career. Helping Pedro was a great pleasure for me, now renewed in light of the turn his career has taken, full of achievements and humanitarian work with high social significance.

10

The Entrepreneurial Dentist

What is vocation? If we look in the dictionary, we will see one entry that defines vocation as the natural and spontaneous disposition that guides a person toward an activity, function, or profession; a penchant, propensity, tendency. It's also defined as something derived by extension of a sense, like any natural aptitude or taste; disposition, inclination, talent.

These were my thoughts when I met Fabio in 2002, a young man who came from a long line of dentists and was quite successful at his profession. However, he still felt something was missing. What could be Fabio's vocation? Could we say that his inclination, like so many members of his family, was for dentistry? It's hard to say. Sometimes we are raised hearing things that we assimilate into our personalities, incorporating them into our life plan in such a way that it becomes impossible to gauge whether we ever really had a choice. Could this profession be a quirk of genetics or just an unconscious obligation for Fabio? The fact is that Fabio, following the path of most of his family, graduated as a dentist after completing the course at the University of São Paulo.

Treating teeth was never, however, the only interest of this young Brazilian of Japanese descent. He also liked to think up new businesses. In addition to his private clinic, where he worked as a dentist and periodontist, he had established a nonprofit organization focused on the prevention of oral diseases through lectures in local schools. He made common cause with many of his colleagues and, at a certain point, realized that the activity, besides helping people, could be profitable. He then devised prevention kits. Although sold at low cost, the large volume ended up generating a significant amount of profit. He later extended his scope of action to general preventive medicine. The business grew and became very successful.

As an officer in his professional association, a partner and administrator of a dental clinic, the founder of an NGO aimed at providing free dental care (with more than a hundred volunteers), an assistant professor of periodontology in graduate and extension courses, he still found time to take a course in management at the Fundação Getúlio Vargas (one of Brazil's strongest business schools). You could say that Fabio was, at the very least, restless. By the time he started producing his dental kits he had already acquired sufficient financial independence to stop treating patients directly.

When he sought me out, he had two problems. He did not think his personal story as a dentist was very fascinating; moreover, he did not want to be away from his responsibilities for too long, and therefore sought an appropriate one-year program. Regarding the first issue, I made him see the beauty of his profession, giving him the tools and awareness to tell his story with the necessary confidence. We then proceeded to address the second issue. Through our contacts at Kellogg, we found out that they offered a one-year MBA option for students with degrees in business administration. We also learned that, because Fabio worked as an administrator and had done a specialization course in business, he qualified to apply for the program. He did apply, was admitted, and earned his MBA within the scheduled single year.

Soon after attaining his MBA in 2004, Fabio returned to his prior activities in Brazil: the dental-health-prevention organization and the dental clinic. He also worked with distant colleagues to create a new company, one based on a business plan that he and a group of Europeans had written while still at Kellogg. The plan aimed to replicate in Europe the business model of the American company Coinstar, basically providing automated, coin-counting services in supermarket chains. It had been a winner in Kellogg's annual entrepreneurship competition, and proved a real-world winner now.

Not content with this success, in late 2004, Fabio bought 50 percent of a small, women's luxury fashion brand based in Recife. In January of 2005, the brand was part of São Paulo Fashion Week, the most important event in the Brazilian fashion world.

Although Fabio never completely abandoned dentistry, I felt that we had a lot in common. In a way, this dentist had, like me, migrated from health care into business. The question about vocation asked at the beginning of the chapter remains, therefore, in my opinion open. Is it possible, or even necessary, for a person with so many skills to choose just one vocation? For Fabio, and for so many like him, the answer is a resounding no.

11

Brancaleone's Army

Every time I think of the 1960s' Italian film comedy *Brancaleone's Army*, I am reminded of the birth of the *MIT Sloan Yearbook*, a project I helped develop during my second-year elective course, Marketing and Advertising. Like the movie's team of underdog misfits, we too managed to emerge triumphant. As the course did not appeal to colleagues interested in finance and related areas, it attracted only about thirty enrollees. Our very first assignment caught us by surprise: a group project to develop a product from scratch. Our grades would be based on the sales success of that product, expressed as a percentage of sales estimated in the project's initial presentation. The groups could be between four and five people and the students could choose their team themselves.

Groups quickly formed, and three students were left without a team—the Australian lawyer Simon, the American artist Beth, and myself. Embarrassed, we sat together in the back, united more by circumstances than by any specific affinity. Simon soon suggested a product that initially struck me as odd and somewhat unexciting: he proposed that we create a class yearbook containing names and pictures of our fellow students, along with paragraphs describing them, a list of professors, and so forth.

I had my misgivings about the choice of product, but apart from that, I felt that a product launch, especially within a marketing class context, should start with market research. Thus, we distributed a questionnaire to colleagues, containing a page from Simon's yearbook.

The main question in the questionnaire was simply "Do you think our class should have a yearbook?"

The overwhelming response was "I couldn't care less." The rejection rate was higher than 85 percent. Simon, an optimist by nature, said that at least 15 percent thought it was a good idea. He argued that some people had even offered to collaborate in the yearbook's preparation. In truth, two volunteers had indeed been sympathetic to the idea of having a post-MBA reminder of their colleagues.

At the next class, we presented the product in its preproject stage, and faced the taunts of colleagues whose ambitious plans included new software, a contraption for slicing burgers, an electronic turnstile, and many other ingenious ideas. The professor did not reject our idea out of hand, but required our marketing plan to include an advertising campaign to improve the numbers we had projected based on our market research. This task became my responsibility, since Simon would be organizing the descriptive paragraphs and Beth would take care of the layout.

Making use of photocopied handouts, lots of creativity and wit, we began to bombard the entire class of two hundred students with our advertising. We put up posters in strategic places around the entire school, even the bathrooms. We got a statement from economics professor Lester Thurow, the renowned author of academic best sellers, saying that our yearbook would be the best book ever written on MIT premises. And so, with intelligent humor, we started to gain sympathy from the class. At one point, people would even ask us on the days when we didn't put up any new ads, "What, no advertising today?" People had started to look forward to our ads!

Gradually, our colleagues accepted the responsibility of writing their stories for our yearbook, becoming committed to the project and enabling the production of a dummy, which we presented to the director of the MBA course, the dreaded Jeff Barks, famous for a policy of cost containment throughout his tenure. We needed money to print the yearbook with sufficient quality in three colors. Since it would be a souvenir for each student, we wanted it to look nice.

To our surprise, the director not only released the funds (US$8,000), but he later wrote a letter praising our initiative and saying that he hoped that the yearbook would become a tradition. The student director, Linda Stantial, wrote a letter saying we had also shown that students with degrees in the humanities could contribute greatly to the MBA class at MIT (a paradigm shift at this school in my time). I cherish this letter and have kept it till today.

In the following pages, I share some of the advertisements that we did, as well as copies of the letters we received praising the initiative. The ads refer to the project's launch and the need to collect photos of each student to publish in the yearbook. In total, we created sixteen different ads over four months, making and distributing about three hundred copies of each.

In 1455,
Gutenberg brought
the miracle of printing
to the civilized world.

531 YEARS LATER, WE ARE BRINGING IT TO SLOAN.

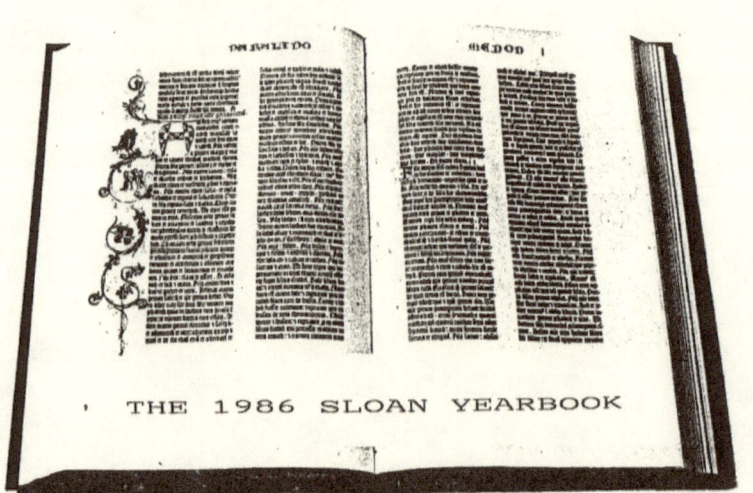

THE 1986 SLOAN YEARBOOK

WE KNOW JUST HOW YOU FEEL.

XV - 86

Some photographs simply don't capture our best side.

Massachusetts Institute of Technology
Alfred P. Sloan School of Management
50 Memorial Drive
Cambridge, Massachusetts 02139

Telephone: 617-253-3747

Jeffrey A. Barks
Associate Dean
Master's and Bachelor's Programs

May 27, 1986

Mr. Ricardo Betti
Mr. Simon J. Dyer
Ms. Beth E. Klingher

Dear Ricardo, Simon, and Beth:

I wanted to formally let you know how impressed I am by the
1986 Sloan Yearbook. As you know I was somewhat skeptical at
the start about the project; you certainly proved me wrong.

Your hard work and creativity have added something special
to this year's commencement. I hope it may become a tradition.

Cordially,

Jeffrey A. Barks

JAB:ch

Placement Office
Room E52-111
Sloan School of Management
Massachusetts Institute of Technology
50 Memorial Drive
Cambridge, Massachusetts 02139

Linda Stantial
Director

Telephone
(617) 253-6149

5/17/86

Dear Beth, Ricardo + Simon —

What a gift you have delivered us! The
yearbook is wonderful — clever, fun,
professional. I appreciate your vision
and stamina. For one thing, you've
provided me with tangible proof of
the non-analytical, non-quantitative
talents of Sloan students.

So, congratulations on such a success.
I'm sure there's lots of pride and
satisfaction you're feeling with your
final product now in hand.

Thank you + rejoice —
Linda

Once we had raised the necessary funds, we began to sell the book at ten dollars per copy. Our approved sales target was two hundred copies. We met the target before even receiving the material from the printing house! It turned out that many people outside our class also wanted to buy the book—teachers, cafeteria staff, and first-year students. We negotiated a second edition with an order for 150 copies, which also sold out. In sum, after discounting the production costs ($8,300), we finished the project with a profit of over $3,000, which we invested in a party in the lobby of the school, complete with barbecue and beer for all students, faculty, and staff. At the party, we distributed the books and received a silver plaque from our classmates, thanking us for a job well done.

More than recognition from our classmates and the director, more than the grade we got (the only project that received an A+), we had the pleasure of being approached during the party by a group of first-year students interested in making another yearbook the following year. An unforeseen by-product, but one that was much celebrated, was the perpetuation of our initiative. It continues to this day, more than two decades later. Every year, when alumni are invited to address groups of interested students about their MIT experience, I'm asked to tell this story—the story of the creation of the yearbook. It helps to demystify the MIT program and shows that there is also space for nonengineers in the course.

In 2006, my wife and I went to my twenty-year reunion at MIT. It was a heck of a party. For three days, we attended classes, workshops, and seminars with some of the most famous speakers at the school. We were also invited to a gala presentation by the Boston Pops symphony orchestra and attended two formal dinners with our former classmates. We had the pleasant experience of meeting people who had graduated five, ten, and fifteen years prior. More than sixty people from my class attended the reunion. We had colleagues come from Australia (Simon, of course), Singapore, Hong Kong, Korea, and other distant countries. To our delight, many brought their copies of the yearbook and were rereading parts of it during the party. The same happened in the 2011 reunion, which coincided with the 150th anniversary of MIT. A major topic of the party was that yearbook.

All MIT alumni were prompted to write a statement about our post-MBA lives on the MIT website. It was a great pleasure for me to write about my career, ending my text as follows:

> The MBA was a turning point in our lives. By nurturing our entrepreneurial spirit and giving us the self-confidence to explore new paths, it strengthened our belief in the future. It is this faith that we insist on sharing with young people seeking our advice.

12

The King of the Waters

Athletes treat their bodies differently from the rest of us. They subject themselves to extreme sacrifices. They learn to live with muscle aches, severe fatigue, all sorts of aggression against their bodies. They give everything of themselves in competitions, and the next day, they show the same dedication in preparing for the next competition or meet. Together with their coaches and trainers, they set ambitious goals—goals that can turn an already difficult routine into a nightmare. They control their weight obsessively to gain precious seconds in speed, and repeat movements tirelessly in search of perfection, always increasing the time spent practicing. If their talent or ability gets them to the first division, either professional or amateur, defending top clubs or the colors of their country, they become gods, their perfect bodies almost temples. They practically become machines that need to be well prepared, always ready, without any hesitation. Injury is their greatest fear, enemy, and threat. Often it is with injury that the dream dies. For an athlete, there is simply nothing worse.

Marcos was an Olympic-level athlete. The invitation to be the goalkeeper of the Brazilian water polo team was the culmination of a great personal battle. It was a wonderful recognition of hours and hours of dedication, miles and miles of swimming. From that moment, the sport, which was already important to him, became the focus of his life. Having spent a year in the army before college, he later decided to abandon his undergraduate business studies at the Fundação Armando Alvares Penteado (FAAP), transferring to an easier school so that he could spend more time practicing, travel whenever necessary, and play water polo around the world without worrying about his studies. The idea was great; he managed to get a college diploma, even though his grades were merely average.

Then he felt a severe pain in his arm. He couldn't defend the goal or hold the ball up; in fact, he could barely swim. He went to speak to the doctor, feeling scared to death. Although his own father was a physician, he dreaded having to see one—in this case, with good reason, for there was a mysterious lump on his arm. He noticed the doctor frowning while examining his elbow. He felt a shiver down his spine.

Then the diagnosis: it was a malignant tumor. Every doctor he saw recommended amputating his arm. In order to survive, Marcos would have to be mutilated. His perfect body would be crippled. His father, a cardiologist, could not accept the prognosis. He took his son to Massachusetts General Hospital, in Boston. The doctors there gave them hope. It would be possible to treat the tumor without amputation. He had good chances for recovery—but no chance to continue as a professional athlete. The game was over, with no chance for reprieve. No national water polo team, no Olympics, no more spectacular saves at the goalpost. It was the end of his sports career.

Thus Marcos's arm was saved, but he found himself without employment opportunities. He decided to return to the aquatic world . . . in a sense. He started marketing mineral water from a source on a property that his family owned. Then he became determined to earn his MBA, and he came to me for help.

After a year-long period of preparation, he applied to Boston University—Boston seemed to be part of his destiny. In his essays, we explored the irony of his past as a water polo player against the present, in which he sold mineral water. We were successful. So much so that BU's magazine published an article about Marcos by the time he attended the MBA program, using the following phrase as a headline: *"Water Polo and Mineral Water Equal Success for MBA."* Beneath the headline was a photo of Marcos beside a pool, holding up a water bottle.

Although not a top-ten school, BU was emerging, with potential to soar in the rankings. Marcos chose the International Management specialization, which consisted of one semester in Japan and a year and a half in Boston. Marcos transferred to his studies all the effort required to succeed as an athlete. He had inaugurated a new phase of his life and a new facet of his personality, devoting himself entirely to excelling as a student.

He ended up getting an excellent job offer from a pharmaceutical laboratory in London for a period of one year. After that, he was invited to work at AB-InBev, where he rapidly advanced to sales executive. Then his career really began to skyrocket. He became director of Nestlé Waters—water again!—and then national manager for ConAgra Foods, a multinational food company that chose Marcos to lead the implementation of its business in Brazil. Next, he joined his older brother in the business of providing services to the São Paulo subway system, with excellent results selling rechargeable subway cards, Paguexpress, to thousands of passengers a day. With every step in his career, he saw a new success.

Where does the explanation lie for such great achievement from someone who had not always attended the best schools? I believe the answer is emotional intelligence. Our former water polo player is a captivating team player who knows how to motivate those around him to give their best. He is also determined to achieve his goals. Importantly, he learned how to take advantage of his classes, absorbing everything he needed to become an effective manager.

According to Marcos, that year he'd spent in the army helped him to develop leadership and discipline, abilities which were also encouraged in water polo. I used to joke with him that our goal was to ensure that he got an interview. From then on, I had no doubt that he would beat the competition. And so it was, not only in gaining admission to do an MBA degree, but in all stages of his career.

13

The Audacious Office Boy

This story, like that of the "King of the Waters" above, is one that greatly moves me, for it recounts the triumph of Romilson, a classic anti-candidate, completely outside the mainstream.

I laughed a lot when Romilson told me about his early career at Banco Itaú in São Paulo, as a fourteen-year-old newcomer from Bahia, in the northeastern region of Brazil. Annoyed with his first day of work as an office boy, he knocked on the marketing director's door and asked to be transferred. No one had told him that such a thing was unthinkable in a company of that size—office boys usually do not speak to directors so unceremoniously. Romilson, however, with the innocence typical of rookies, especially coming from a less-developed part of the country, thought he had the right to invade the director's office and tell him, "I would like to work in your area, because I want to be a marketing professional. Are there any positions for me?"

The executive was so amused by the boy's boldness and optimism that he decided to give him a chance. After that day, Romilson proudly began to present himself as the marketing office boy. Eventually, he made a career in marketing, climbing every step of the ladder until he reached the position of manager. It did not happen overnight, of course; it took sixteen years of hard work.

His first step was to combine study and work. While working at Itaú during the day he also attended night school to get a degree in business at the University of São Paulo.

This story of resilience alone would be enough for him to get into several good MBA programs, but Romilson wanted to go to the best marketing school in the world—Kellogg. He already had an offer of sponsorship from the bank to pay for the course. It would be up to me to guide him on how best to position himself against the competition.

In our first interview, it became clear to me that we should tell the story of the audacious office boy, but I wanted to add other good stories to his application. It seemed to me that the case of the boy who knew what he wanted and fought to achieve it, while important, was already a little distant in time since it happened when he was just fourteen. We needed more recent achievements. That was when he came out with another gem—*the* one, in my opinion—which was crucial to his gaining admitted to Kellogg, despite not having a very high GMAT score.

It so happened that Romilson had the responsibility to interface with the company's advertising agencies. On one occasion, he questioned an agency's choice regarding how to advertise a bank service to retired people. The ad showed the Brazilian composer and singer Dorival Caymmi swaying in a hammock under a brilliant sun, surrounded by coconut trees, enjoying a lazy idleness. The product's subsequent performance, however, was not satisfactory: it languished at twelfth in national rankings.

Guided by Romilson, the agency built a new campaign, using a different strategy. The ads now showed four retirees in good shape—Sean Connery among them—going into the sea with their surfboards. The message was totally different. Inactivity had been exchanged for activity, health, energy, and other positive attributes associated with that group of retirees. In less than eleven months, the product rose to first place in the Brazilian rankings. I liked this story so much that I insisted that he include in his essay two illustrations of the commercials, a sort of "Before and After Romilson."

It was clear to me that Romilson should go personally to the interview at Kellogg in the United States, even though they offered the possibility of doing the interview in Brazil with local alumni. But our candidate had a tight budget, making such plans difficult. I appealed to my former clients for help. I got in touch with Pedro, whose story is detailed above in "The Brazilian Rock Star," and Ricardo G., whose story is not detailed in these pages. Both were studying at Kellogg at the time. I asked them to arrange free lodging for Romilson, which they happily did. In the end, his only expense was the airplane ticket, and he got a good deal on that. It was a quick trip, just to do the interview.

My point in advising him to go there was that, with such an engaging personality and with such an unusual background in Brazil, Romilson could profitably present himself to the admissions officer without intermediaries. I could imagine the scene in my mind: the strong, friendly, talkative dark-skinned man with an earring in his ear, coming straight from Brazil to speak directly with a key decision maker. Just as the brash, fourteen-year-old Romilson had impressed his marketing director, I felt confident that his stories and character would prove memorable to the interviewer. We planned the interview so that he could show the pictures of "Before and After Romilson," which had been included in his application package. We could not be sure that the interviewer had seen them. He took colored copies in his luggage.

The next day, I almost fell out of bed when I received a late-night phone call from the United States. Once the interview was over, Romilson said he could not wait—he needed to tell me how it went.

Screaming and crying, he said, "I got into Kellogg! I'm sure of it!" It turned out that the interviewer had wanted to keep the pictures. Romilson had told her that the originals were in the application package, but she had replied that she wanted the copies to take home to show her kids!

Bingo! That was it. We had hooked the interviewer. The anti-candidate had just won a place in the Mecca of marketers. He went there and showed Philip Kotler, Kellogg's international marketing guru, what a *Bahiano* has got to offer, as the well-known song by Carmem Miranda goes.

14

The Tailor's Pen

Some business schools ask very subjective questions in their applications. They encourage candidates to share feelings and emotions, show their sensitivity, reveal the more pronounced traits of their personalities.

In the case of Stanford Graduate School of Business, for example, the application is practically a therapy session. It is with that spirit and intention that they ask their main question: "What matters most to you?" Easy, right? And there is no demonstrated concern about candidates expressing themselves succinctly. The space is sufficient for candidates to stretch their thoughts out, so long as they respect the limit of three to eight pages of text.

At Berkeley's Haas School of Business, on the other hand, there was an oft-asked question with a different slant on psychology: "What is your most important tangible possession?" How would you respond to this? Someone in a rush might respond listing material properties of monetary value. I believe that our immediate response is to list homes, cars, or something along those lines—things that can be priced. We would then be responding directly to what was being asked, mechanically following the instructions. However, this question is less straightforward than it seems. We would have to, in referring to the tangible possession, go a bit further. Associate it with a larger and more subjective dimension. The possession must be tangible and measurable, but its importance should be intangible and personal.

My client Osmar captured this nuance very well, producing a masterful response to the question. I have no doubt that his understanding of the question and his exceptional response were decisive in his admission to Berkeley. This is the story he told me:

> The scissors cut the cloth smoothly, sharply, gliding over the straight line that had been drawn with care, a quick opening-and-closing of blades, a steady hand very familiar with the tool it was gripping. One more piece that would later be joined and stitched at the appropriate place to create the suit that had been ordered. Pants and jacket made to measure.
>
> The tailor stretched his arms. He distracted himself by listening to the music playing softly in the background. He felt indecisive, wanting to get up and increase the volume, yet postponing the decision, too tired to rise. He massaged his sore neck. Despite his fatigue, he felt content. The business was going well. The old radio, his friend, practically a partner in his craft, present every day of his life, had the means to energize him. He could not survive without it. Music, news, food for the heart and mind. An antidote to the loneliness of the repetitive work.
>
> The shrill sound of the doorbell made him finally decide. He put on his shoes and, feeling his bones ache, snapped the radio off, going to answer the door and admit his client.
>
> The mirror revealed his mastery. It was a perfect fit. Two joys: a service well done and a service well compensated. The tailor handed the client a gold fountain pen with which to sign the check. His expression revealed his pride in owning that pen. He had saved up a long time to buy it. It was his single luxury. He watched the letters taking shape on the paper, validating the check. The check was recognition of the quality of his work. The pen glittered in the light as he received it back.

I was moved when he told me about his grandfather, the tailor. The old man had saved money for years to buy that gold fountain pen. Proudly, almost as a ritual, he offered it to clients to sign their checks for the clothes he had made them. The old man's dream had been to see his son earn a college degree. With much effort, working long hours for years, he managed to achieve that goal. Osmar's father graduated in economics at the University of São Paulo and had a brilliant career.

Later, Osmar repeated the feat, completing the same course at the same university, becoming an economist working in the financial market. As his inheritance from his grandfather, he received the treasured gold fountain pen. To Osmar, the pen symbolized his grandfather's struggle to rise in social stature, the battle of a tailor to ensure a better future for his children and grandchildren. A pen that was full of meaning.

After completing his MBA at Berkeley, Osmar became one of the school's representatives in Brazil. He is still doing very well in the financial market. Every time we meet, I remember the story about the pen. Certainly, the admissions officer who read his application remembers as well.

15

Culture Shock

No one goes to school abroad without facing major issues outside of the MBA program itself. The fear of culture shock often poses as much of a challenge for my clients as the academic courses ahead of them. They expect the differences in language, religion, socioeconomic ideology, philosophy, moral values, ethics—in short, everything that characterizes the identity of a group of people of a certain nationality—to hamper their ability to adjust. In practice, however, when we leave Brazil to study in more developed countries, the differences we thought were so profound tend to become unimportant in day-to-day life within a student community. Indeed, the social arrangement in that kind of microcosm is usually so efficient that our adaptation is much easier than we expect it to be, allowing us to take full advantage of the experience of living abroad. However, no one escapes completely. So to ease my clients' anxiety, I often share a few amusing stories of my own adjustment.

After some time living in Massachusetts, I had started to admire many qualities of that environment so filled with college students (there are more than forty colleges in Boston alone), where words are valuable and knowledge is the main currency. As with any new experience, my first months required a lot of flexibility and patience, until I absorbed the customs of a society very different from my own. I inevitably committed many *faux pas* that I later regretted, but eventually, I just accepted such errors as part of the continuous learning that is life.

In the initial months of new circumstances—when we have to incorporate the slang, when the codes of etiquette are not yet explicit, when the *modus vivendi* of those around us are still foreign—our peace of mind depends largely on the attitude with which we face the unavoidable embarrassing moments. Good humor is a prerequisite for this phase; we collect funny stories that will yield good laughs for the rest of our lives.

I remember with mirth some of these episodes, which my wife, Sandra, and I have recounted to our children and certainly will tell our grandchildren as well. In one such episode, on the second day after we had moved into an apartment on the MIT campus, Sandra decided to do the spring cleaning before furnishing the house. She filled a bucket with water, mixed some cleaner into the water, and poured the mix onto the living room floor. To our amazement, and utterly unlike any dwelling in Brazil, there was no drain to remove the water anywhere in the apartment! Not even in the bathrooms and laundry area! We spent hours drying the floor with towels, frustrated by our mistake. Then we discovered that all campus buildings were like that, and that floor cleaning here was done with mops. No American would ever dream of throwing a bucket of water on the floor of his or her home!

Another interesting story involved the hand brake on our first American car. We had bought a Dodge for three thousand dollars and parked it outdoors, since our building had no garage. It wasn't a problem when we arrived in the fall. But then winter came and, with it, the first snowfall. When I went to leave for campus in the morning, after clearing the path with a shovel, I started the engine, but the car would not move. The hand brake was locked! There I was, late for class, not knowing what to do until I saw a neighbor laughing at my misfortune. He explained that most people with cars that stayed outdoors in the winter left their hand brakes off. This prevents the brake cable from freezing in the activated position. I would either have to wait for warmer weather, call a mechanic with an acetylene torch to melt the ice on the cable, or proceed to school on foot in the snow. I chose the latter path, and my more experienced classmates confirmed the diagnosis. The next day, the weather warmed, the brake loosened up, and I put the problem behind me. But I learned my lesson, and never again set the hand brake in the winter. Luckily I didn't have to park on a hill!

On another winter's day, I went shopping at a grocery store while Sandra took care of the children. Returning to the car, I came upon a homeless woman sitting on the hood. I often stumbled over words in

English and did not want to offend the woman, so I made a great effort to be polite as I told her, "I am sorry to misplace you, but I have to go home."

To my relief, she was not angry. Instead, she gathered her bags with resignation, got off the hood, and went off to sit on another car, certainly seeking to warm herself with the heat of its engine. Before she departed, she turned to me and shouted one word: "Displace!" I was puzzled until I realized that she was correcting my English. Of course she had understood me, but had decided not to let it slide. I felt like I should thank her and extend a coin for the English lesson.

I will share just one more faux pas vignette before getting back to the MBA discussion. On a sunny Sunday in early spring during the MBA program, after a long and stressful winter, Sandra and I decided to take our children and find a good place for a picnic and a swim. We encountered a large lake, surrounded by a pleasant forest, with the inviting name of Fresh Pond. We did not hesitate. We stopped right there and proceeded toward the lake with all the accessories that we had brought for the occasion: buoys, buckets, shovels, flippers, bathing suits, towels, drinks, and sandwiches. When we got closer, though, our way was blocked by a wire fence, so we asked a man who was jogging nearby, "Where is the entrance?" to which he replied, "Entrance to where?" And we explained, "To the lake, of course!"

He looked stunned, measured us up and down, and asked incredulously, "You want to *swim* in Fresh Pond?" We all nodded affirmatively and enthusiastically. Amazed, he explained that that would be impossible. This was the city's water reservoir, and swimming was therefore, of course, forbidden. We returned home defeated, and, after that, always investigated more diligently before going off on local adventures. The man must have gotten a good laugh at the crazy Brazilians who wanted to swim in the reservoir! We also laugh about it to this day; the whole episode has become a family joke.

Beyond these anecdotes, I remember a few occasions I would call genuine culture shock, especially as concerns the relationship between men and women in the university environment. In 1984, when I got to MIT, the female students were still fighting for their independence, but were years ahead of Brazilian women. Some were angry or defensive when confronting men. At first, I would open doors or let them into the elevator first, niceties I learned early on in Brazil. But this courtesy was often misinterpreted by the American women. In the elevator or anywhere that had a queue, the inflexible rule was "First come, first serve." Opening doors for a woman was likely to be met with the phrase, "Please do not patronize me." I ended up changing my ways and learned to dance to the local music. When I got back to Brazil, I had to retrain myself to go back to my old manners, albeit now with a new awareness.

16

All for a Harley-Davidson

Dárcio was an engineer who was to be sponsored by his employer for the MBA. At first glance, his story did not seem that unusual. Engineers working in large banks in the area of telecommunications are quite common. But not like Dárcio. As hard as he tried, the person sitting opposite me simply did not fit the pattern that I was used to seeing. He was a different kind of person in every way, and it was exactly on his uniqueness that we relied to beat the odds.

Anyone who has worked in a bank knows the conservatism of these institutions. Nothing too obvious, the standards are not always written. The way one presents oneself, behaves, or dresses is something you would not find in any guidebook, manual, or explicit guideline. Common sense ends up creating the rules, and the intuition of each employee defines what is right and wrong. Dark suits, mostly white shirts, ties, clean-shaven faces, and polished shoes thus become almost an obligation. One employee copies another. These copies have, over time, defined the banker way of being.

Dárcio fled all that . . . shall we say . . . boredom. He sported a big earring, tattoos, a shaved head, and a leather jacket. I think if he worked in other areas of the bank and had a different personality, he might have eventually changed his look. The telecom team, however, always seemed more flexible. To complement the look, he presented himself with a consistent attitude: *strong*. A challenger, he defended his opinions with sound arguments, but almost angrily.

When I heard that he had participated in an exchange program in the United States, spoke English fluently, and had specialized in an area that required deep technical knowledge, I began to understand that those external signs were a form of disguise. I actually had in front of me someone determined and ambitious. Always determined to chase his dreams, he had saved his allowance since adolescence with the firm purpose of someday buying a Harley-Davidson motorcycle. His parents, middle-class people, could not give him what he wanted. A motorbike was an expensive luxury for them. He told me how he came to have a passion for motorbikes:

> *Easy Rider*, 1969. Two modern cowboys mounted on their bikes, riding aimlessly. Peter Fonda and Dennis Hopper living like Billy the Kid and Jesse James. Sitting in the comfortable chair of the cinema, seeing the famous old movie, I imagined the wind on the face of the protagonists . . . that feeling of freedom spoken out loud, pounding in my head rhythmically to the sound of the band Steppenwolf, playing "Born to be Wild." It awoke the passion for motorcycling in me. I wanted to enter the screen and become a hero.
>
> Riding a Harley chopper, I let my imagination put me in the middle of the film. I was Billy and Jesse and Peter and Dennis all at the same time, an American hero wandering the roads with no worries or boundaries. Without limits; sex, drugs, and rock 'n' roll. I almost imitated Jane's brother's famous gesture. I also wanted to throw my wristwatch to the ground. Be free of hours passing by. Ignore time. Racing on the Harley, I would live in the supremacy of being myself. I would speak, think, and act as I saw fit. I would not feel fear.
>
> I realized that we are not afraid of people, but only of what they represent. Freedom scares everybody. It is very hard to be free when we can be bought and sold. But never accuse someone of not being free. It is an accusation that could infuriate anyone.
>
> Influenced by the classic movie, I saw society crumbling under standardized behavior. There are movies that stay forever in our hearts. This one marked me. I would always strive to be free and true to my nature. And one day, I would have a Harley.

Of course Dárcio got what he wanted as an adult. In his essays, we recounted the thrill of entering the store and buying his dream motorcycle. We explored the sacrifices he'd made to buy it. Thus, he described himself as an individual accustomed to drinking from all sources: By day, at work, implementing Voice-Over Internet Protocol (VOIP) projects. At night, cruising the streets on his Harley, a proud member of the Harley Owners Group, the HOG.

I wondered what kind of conversations he had with his bearded and tattooed friends who spoke in monosyllables. But Dárcio helped me see that my way of thinking was prejudiced. All kinds of people were part of HOG, all of them united by the dream of having a Harley. As I got to know him, I was not surprised when I learned that Dárcio was also a DJ and composer in his spare time and had written a song that won the iBest prize on the Internet. I got used to the wide horizons of my atypical "typical" client.

At crunch time, everything worked out. He got a great score on the GMAT and, with the excellent example of determination described in his essays, was admitted to no less an institution than Wharton, one of the best business schools in the world. Today he is back in Brazil and works at the bank that sponsored his course. He still dresses as he sees fit, though, and of course still rides his Harley.

17

The Guy Who Had Been Expelled

Some years after I returned from MIT, I noticed that my spoken English was getting rusty. It is amazing how quickly we lose our proficiency with languages! So I decided to enroll in advanced courses in English conversation, the arts, American history, and contemporary events. This healthy habit not only allowed me to recover the old fluency, but also broadened my general knowledge and my circle of friends.

In one of these courses, I ran into Paulo B. Young, studious, a bit shy, but very intelligent. He had a good level of English comprehension and became interested in my work, for he had thought of doing an MBA someday. At the end of the semester, when we said good-bye, I gave him my business card.

After some years, he came to see me at my office. He had matured. He came with the firm intention of studying abroad. He immediately warned me, however, about a problem in his transcript that had plagued him for years. He feared that it was severe enough to remove him from contention for the best MBA schools. He had been expelled from his engineering course!

Upon hearing which school he had been expelled from, I became quite worried, for this was a college with a strong military influence, and rigid values of discipline, respect, and responsibility. If his situation was poorly explained or poorly resolved, if there was any doubt left about the real reasons for his expulsion, the dream of a first-rate school abroad would definitely be compromised. But there was no way we could omit this fact. It was recorded in the school transcripts, which were required as part of the application.

As always, there was a story to be told. Upon hearing what Paulo B. had to say I realized that the expulsion could work in our favor. The facts were very clear: He had been a good student who had decided to do a period abroad during his engineering course. As there were no programs at the time for going abroad at the institution where he was studying, he decided to take time off and go to France. There, he would gain international experience, learn another language, and broaden his cultural horizons.

He achieved his goals. He worked for one year in a car factory, studied languages, and traveled whenever possible. He actually went beyond his original goals. He approached a prestigious local college and managed to convince them to create an exchange program with his university. The idea was to bring students from his school in Brazil to France, starting that very year. He returned to Brazil feeling quite enthusiastic. He was proud of having been able to create for his colleagues the same opportunities for intellectual growth that he had just enjoyed.

Unfortunately, the leaders of his school in Brazil did not see the facts the same way. They accused him of using the name of the institution without authorization and said they did not have the slightest interest in that kind of initiative. They argued that there had been no point in interrupting his course for a year or disrupting the curriculum. Surprised by the reaction he encountered, the good student lost his temper. He argued hotheadedly, going beyond certain limits, confronting the sacred precepts of the quasi-military hierarchy of the school. As a result, he was expelled for insubordination.

Not content to accept his fate, Paulo B. hired a lawyer to defend him. After much struggle, he was offered a deal. He would have to recant before the board of directors of the school. If he accepted the offer, he would be reinstated to the course. He accepted. He then concluded the course with terrific grades, but was not allowed to erase the episode from his transcript.

In my view, this story would be enough to justify the record in his transcript, without imposing a risk of damaging his image with the majority of MBA schools. Meanwhile, Paulo B. had achieved a very high score on the GMAT and wanted to get into the most competitive school, Stanford GSB. We needed something else to swing the odds decidedly in his favor.

We found the answer in his family background. Paulo B. told me that his father was a former priest who spent many years fighting to convince the Vatican to recognize his marriage. With this story, suddenly our path was lit. There was an undeniable parallel between the stories of Paulo B. and his father. Both had fought against the institutions to which they belonged in order to defend their rights and their autonomy. In symbolic terms, the story of the small against the great, the ordinary citizen against the system, had repeated itself. Like his father, Paulo B. had overcome significant hurdles through strength of character and the courage of his convictions.

It was another story that ended with much celebration.

18

The Mutant

All change requires courage, and all career change entails risk. The better-run businesses learned this long ago. They are usually the ones with the greatest zeal for their staff, those who know that human capital is the most important asset in a company. In a highly competitive world, in which constant challenges require profound changes in organizational structures, and where such changes may often mean the very survival of the business, those who suffer most are the employees. Their responsibilities are constantly changed, and they have incessant demands placed upon them. It is natural for employees to be driven to distress. They need the monitoring, guidance, and special care that only the best-managed corporations are to provide.

Even at that, few of us easily accept new ways, different management models, real leaps in the dark. We tend to regard our work as something immutable. We want guarantees. We like to think we know our work well, that we are good at what we do, and will continue doing what we have learned to do for a long time.

In my many years working as a consultant, I have learned to respect those who have the knack to adapt easily. Some people simply do not let the laws of inertia conduct their lives. They carry in their minds, their attitudes, a bit of pioneering spirit carried forward from ancestors. They are always ready to experiment, apt to enjoy the new without fear of the unknown.

Every time I remember Otavio's story, it makes me happy. It is always gratifying to participate in important moments in people's lives. In his case, the feeling is even better because I'm sure I instilled in Otavio the confidence that allowed him to get ahead.

It was a complicated case. Otavio had not taken conventional paths. He had gotten a degree in agronomy—the science of soil management, land cultivation, and crop production—entered the financial market, worked in a brokerage house, played the role of agronomist, done amateur theater, and dreamed of having his own business. Such were the multiplicity of his interests and ability to learn new things that he had not moved in a consistent direction. He changed course constantly in the search for personal and professional fulfillment.

As I always do with such clients, I discussed with him this apparent lack of focus, and how it could impact the results of his MBA applications. We concluded that we could try to address this diversity of interests as a point in his favor.

It was always very pleasant to talk to Otavio. Thanks to the vast general knowledge he had, our conversations always took interesting turns. We talked about literature, theater, cinema, arts, and history. Moreover, he had traveled to several countries and had accumulated broad international experience. Culture was not what he lacked.

Nonetheless, we all have flaws. Otavio had a habit of demeaning himself, minimizing the strengths of his personality, and amplifying the negative. That said, I noticed a very special glow in his eyes whenever he spoke of the amateur theater group to which he belonged. I asked him to write about the experience. He completed the assignment masterfully—but not in his eyes. He criticized his essay before showing it to me. He said it was a terrible draft and that I should discount it.

The text began, "*Merde.*" Just like that, *shit* in French. He then described the moment that preceded his entry on stage: doing his makeup before the mirror in the dressing room. It was the way he found to capture the reader's attention. As he described the thrill of being an actor, he explained that *merde* is the universal word actors use to wish each other good luck before going onstage (except in the United States, where people say, "Break a leg!").

Overcoming Otavio's self-doubt, I judged the writing extraordinarily well-crafted, *merde* and all, and insisted that he use it in his applications, predicting a good outcome. And that's what happened. Even with only an average GMAT, he was admitted to the school he wanted, Kellogg, ranked number one in *Business Week* that year and recognized worldwide as the best school for marketing.

After receiving his MBA, and back in Brazil, Otavio remained restless. He became an Internet entrepreneur, rising to president of a well-known online auction company. He later changed fields again, opening a film production company called Mutant Films, a more than appropriate name when it comes to our Otavio. The new enterprise is already going strong, having to date produced many documentaries and various innovative projects.

I pay tribute to this courageous mutant, the only person in my experience who had the nerve to write *merde* in his application and make it work. *Merde* to you too, Otavio!

19

The Jungle Boy

No, I don't have a new path. What I have is a new way of walking.

—Thiago de Mello

This phrase from the Amazon poet Thiago de Mello always puts me in a reflective mood. I think they are wise words with a broad meaning. Besides moving me with its beauty, it impresses me as a message, one that I routinely share with my clients. We must seek new ways of walking.

Thiago de Mello demonstrated this in his own life. He was born in the Amazon in 1926 and moved to Rio de Janeiro to study medicine. Torn between medical science and poetic art, he took the courageous step (especially for that time) of choosing poetry over medicine. If one can grant that there is poetry in consulting, then my own path, in a way, mirrors his.

The fascination that foreigners have for the Amazon is incredible. It is different from what I feel for the area. It is a place which for me has a charm that comes from childhood, when my readings about Greek mythology populated my dreams. Women warriors dedicated to hunting and war, who amputated their right breasts (hence the name Amazon, which in Greek means *no breasts*) to better handle a bow. It is also, of course, the name of the longest river in the world, so named by Francisco de Orellana in 1542 while he was being attacked by a tribe of Indians coming down the river. He judged these people to be warrior women—hence the river's name.

The world looks to the Amazon region with less romantic eyes. They see beyond the forest's wealth of natural beauty. They measure the potential in the livestock sector, and of the vast mineral resources and large hydroelectric capacity. They know it is more than a priceless ecological reserve; the region is also "the lungs of the world."

Whenever I encounter clients from that part of Brazil, those with rainforest roots, I encourage them to explore their origins in their applications. It has been a surefire recipe for awakening the interest of admissions officers. One such case happened with Joney, who had lived in São Paulo since coming from the north to take his degree in engineering at the renowned Instituto Tecnológico de Aeronáutica (ITA).

Joney's life story is very interesting. It begins with his childhood in the Amazon, where the young boy, belonging to a group of Boy Scouts, found it an ideal setting for small boys to live big adventures. It was common, he told me, to make excursions into the jungle's interior.

I could not help imagining myself in those situations. It must have been wonderful. I think every adventurous child growing up in a big city, far from a place like the Amazon, dreams of camping in the forest, belonging to an organized tribe, defying the dangers and mysteries hidden in the woods. The stories he told me were wondrous, full of situations straight out of films. Poisonous snakes, wild animals, jaguars, monkeys, and colorful birds. Clouds of insects, haunted nights, traps, encounters with indigenous people, and tropical storms. Hunting, fishing, a whole universe inhabited by that boy who knew all the streams by name.

He did well in his high school studies and eventually moved to Rio de Janeiro, aiming to better prepare for the college admission exam. At the same time he had to overcome a series of family problems that persisted throughout his university years. These issues became so serious that he ended up having to assume full responsibility for the domestic affairs of his relatives. This all happened very early, at a time when most people still receive support and encouragement from their parents.

Hearing the details of Joney's story, I could better understand the meaning of breadwinner, having before only interpreted it from the financial point-of-view. I now understood the word's many meanings: one who puts in order, arranges, protects, supports, cares for, maintains. Joney was, from a young age, the family counselor, the psychological mainstay, the financial consultant, the conflict resolver and, finally, the bearer of an enormous responsibility that made him mature very early.

Joney's early maturity and determination to get ahead led him to move to São Paulo, where his career opportunities would be greater. He soon got international consulting work, and his innate leadership skills were quickly noticed. He progressed rapidly. The positive reviews he received, as well as the excellent letters of recommendation, enabled his rapid career ascension and later enriched his MBA application. Even at that, I am convinced that his Amazonian past sparked the interest of admissions officials and won him many points in the diversity category.

The transposition of this beautiful story to paper was key for him to be admitted to MIT and other top schools. The path he took was crowned by success. Upon completion of the course he was hired by a multinational corporation based in Miami. From the rainforest to a great American metropolis: no doubt, a long road traveled by our "jungle boy," with his new way of walking.

20

United by the MBA

One issue I am often consulted about is the possibility of two people applying as a couple to the same MBA program. Over the years, I have helped some couples to accomplish this feat, though it has often turned out much harder than one would think.

Three such stories are worth recounting, because of the special qualities surrounding each candidate-pair.

Alexandre was a physician trained at the University of São Paulo, specializing in orthopedics, and a partner in an orthopedic clinic in São Paulo. He was nearing thirty when he came to me. I immediately identified with the path he had followed, despite the gap of almost twenty years between us. Besides having gone to the same school, we had both participated in the Medicine Show (a comedy show that is still carried out by students at the University of São Paulo Medical School), done military service at the army's general hospital, and had decided to attain an MBA en route to changing professions. The person who told Alexandre about my services was one of his childhood friends, Tomé, a former client of mine who was also a doctor and had become an international executive in the field of medical insurance after completing an MBA at Washington University in St. Louis, Missouri.

Alexandre's girlfriend, Mariana, also wanted to do an MBA degree, despite being younger and having far less professional experience than her future husband. They planned to marry before starting the course. They wanted to get into the same school, or into schools close to each other. My biggest concern was for her, for I knew that her lack of experience would count against her. We nevertheless had hope that some schools would accept her work internships as professional experience and decide to bet on her potential. We decided to explore in depth the details of those internships, highlighting the differences of this type of training in Brazil and the United States. In particular, in Brazil, an intern works practically full-time and is given specific responsibilities, gaining work experience before even graduating from university.

The strategy paid off at the University of North Carolina at Chapel Hill, a reputable MBA program. Both of them were admitted there but Alexandre ended up choosing Duke University, which offered better opportunities in the area of health-care management and, located in neighboring Durham, was close enough to Chapel Hill. Thus, the couple achieved their objective of completing their MBAs in tandem. I got very emotional at their wedding, seeing how they were happy and motivated to grow together.

*   *   *

Another case that struck me, though for different reasons, was a couple who had not reached their goal in the first attempt. Silvio and Fernanda had very different profiles. Although they both worked in the financial market, Silvio had a degree in agronomy and Fernanda in engineering. At the time, Fernanda had greater fluency in English than Silvio, a fact that was reflected in their GMAT scores, undermining their chances of joint approval. Nonetheless, they had almost succeeded. They were on waiting lists and were called for interviews in the United States, but unfortunately their first attempt did not achieve the desired result.

On such occasions, when admission is not attained, we direct clients to investigate with the schools the reasons for not being admitted. This helps us better prepare our reapplication strategy.

Silvio and Fernanda followed this advice and entered the next year's application process much better prepared for the competition. They had gotten higher scores on the GMAT and, as working professionals, now had new achievements to show. It was enough. They were admitted to several schools, but chose Tuck School of Business at Dartmouth College in New Hampshire, as the one that best fit their goals. I was also at their wedding ceremony and celebrated with them the result that certainly changed their lives.

At the end of the course, they both got good jobs in American companies and are currently residing in the United States. It was very gratifying to see them again recently at a Tuck event I attended. The two traveled up to Hanover, New Hampshire, on a weekend so we could meet up and see and tour the city together and attend the graduation of their friends and my clients Guilherme and Juliana, who had employment at Morgan Stanley in New York already lined up. The enthusiasm of all of them to show me that splendid university was only comparable to the shine in the eyes of Silvio telling me about Fernanda's pregnancy.

Over the years, I became a friend of Fernanda's family. I met her parents and advised her younger sister, who ended up getting her MBA at Harvard, as well as her younger brother, Jorge, who did his MBA at MIT.

*   *   *

Finally, I would like to tell the story that inspired the title of this chapter. Nicolas and Renata, two former students of the Getulio Vargas Foundation, had been in love with each other since their college days. They followed different professional paths and eventually were geographically separated, although they maintained a long-distance relationship. Renata moved to the United States and worked for a company based in Seattle, while Nicolas combined his entrepreneurial talent with the phenomenon of Internet startups, creating a website called Oba Oba, which contained information about nightlife in Brazil and was quite popular among young people.

The three of us interacted mostly through conference calls. Discussing the material to use for their applications, it seemed clear that the MBA course would be a great opportunity to get them back together. It was imperative that they go to the same school, or at least the same city. I sensed that the story of two years' dating at a distance would have to be told, for, really, nobody can resist a good love story. Making things easier, the two protagonists had excellent academic backgrounds and all the qualifications desired by the most demanding schools, including high scores on the GMAT. Plus, they had complementary profiles and would not be competing against one another for limited program space.

Their story seduced admissions officers from several of the best schools. They had the privilege of deciding from among many offers where to study and (finally!) live together. They chose, to my delight, MIT, where I had studied. At the MIT Sloan Club of Brazil, we will have our ongoing contact guaranteed for many years. As alumni, we will be able to speak of this school that has the power to transform people's lives.

21

From Cascavel to Vancouver

Sometimes, just for fun, I wonder how it would be to translate some names of Brazilian cities into English and what impact these translations would have on an American reader. One name that always caught my attention was Cascavel, which means rattlesnake in English. In Brazil, we are used to associating that word with the city in western Parana State. There is no immediate connection with the venomous snake. For foreigners, however, the word *rattlesnake* evokes threats in Westerns, cheats, or the nicknames of gangsters—anything except the name of a city.

Coincidentally, one of my clients, Theo, was born in Cascavel. I was impressed when he told me that during his adolescence he had decided to learn English and went on an exchange program to the city of Vancouver in Canada. I soon realized that his initiative to journey from Cascavel to Vancouver, which had represented for him the discovery of new horizons and expansion of future prospects in addition to gains in academic stature, could be used as one of the strengths in his application, helping him to stand out.

I'll make a parenthesis here. International experience is always considered an advantage by institutions of higher learning. People tend to interpret the world through a very limited vision. Many spend their entire lives without ever leaving their neighborhoods or cities, seldom going abroad or even learning very much about their own countries. When we don't travel much, we hardly take notice of our own culture and stop relating with other cultures at all. We ignore the rich diversity of customs, languages, cuisines, and traditions that are spread across continents. We become impoverished as individuals. Those who have spent time in other regions, speaking more than one language, studying, working, or even simply moving across borders by car or train, backpacks on their backs, greatly increase their chances of gaining admission to MBA programs. They are seen as distinguished beings. More open, capable, independent, resourceful; in short, better prepared.

Theo's story was full of academic and professional achievements. Although we could not prove the fact, he probably was the first student from his school in Cascavel to be admitted to Fundação Getúlio Vargas, besides being one of the first to study abroad during high school. During college, he had gone to live in the house of his aunt, who had married the writer and politician Fernando Moraes, in São Paulo.

To make a long story short, for years, the former congressman had shelved a book project, a work that would later become famous. It was an extensive research on the life of Assis Chateaubriand, an influential public figure from the early twentieth century in Brazil, nicknamed Chatô. While living with the young nephew who left his hometown with the firm determination of getting ahead in life, the writer's interest in the project reawakened. They had long evenings full of endless conversations about the character's life. These conversations, besides inspiring Theo to persist in his goals, motivated the author to résumé writing. Moraes's wonderful letter of recommendation, describing Theo's influence on him to finish the book that became a best seller, *Chatô*, was the final touch in a winning application that got him into Kellogg, opening the doors to an international career.

22

The Man Who Inspired a Case Study

One of the things I most appreciate in my work is the opportunity to meet interesting people. Being sought every year by dozens of young people passionate about studying abroad, I often run into unusual people with fascinating qualities or life histories. One of those people was Philip. His strong personality captivated me from our first meeting on. I soon realized that he did not really need my help, but he insisted on visiting me a few times to exchange ideas and show me his essays.

At one point, he showed me a letter from the University of São Paulo, where he had majored in economics, testifying that he had obtained the highest grade-point average in the history of the college. In addition, he had worked at first-rate companies in the areas of strategic consulting and investment banking, but soon came to the conclusion that he had a vocation as an entrepreneur and that the MBA would help prepare him to start his own business.

I remember that he got a high score on the GMAT, 710, but was not satisfied with it, although I assured him that it would be enough to get him into any school. He repeated the test and got a 750. In the end, he sent applications to only two schools, Harvard and Stanford, and was admitted to both, opting for the latter.

Besides showing excellent academic performance, Philip demonstrated strong leadership and great creativity, taking unusual initiatives in life that greatly enriched his story. One was a negotiation with a group of homeless people who had invaded his family's land in the state of Maranhão in northern Brazil. He was very young at the time, still a university student. He traveled from São Paulo to distant

Maranhão and persuaded the group to relocate to another section of the property, away from the area that the family planned to farm in the near future. It was a peaceful solution that accommodated the interests of all involved.

This same persuasiveness appeared in several other episodes he described in his application. Any person who interviewed Philip would be impressed with his reasoning abilities. Later, through other clients who went to Stanford, I heard another story about Philip during the MBA course, and I found it endearing and quite amusing. During a competition involving a series of tasks to be accomplished by teams of students, there was a task that was worth many points: finding people with navel rings. The points would be multiplied by the number of people brought in. Philip convinced his own teammates to get navel rings, thus winning the competition.

After he'd won his degree, Philip accomplished one of the goals discussed in his essays: he launched a shrimp-farming company in northeastern Brazil. It had a promising start and had begun to open a unit in California. When unexpected problems with his partners forced him to shut the expansion down, he regarded the experience as one more learning opportunity and was able to make lemonade out of lemons. Eventually, the episode was published as a case study in the prestigious *Harvard Business Review*, helping to convey valuable lessons for future entrepreneurs.

23

The Russian Prince

In my work, I have to be very careful with first impressions. I cannot always rely directly on the assessments that I make when I meet someone new. Meeting people is not always a simple thing. The natural tendency that we all have is to try to guess about the character of an individual based solely on appearances. This can be dangerously misleading. If I indulge in immediate impressions, subject to the whims of often inexplicable sympathies, I run a serious risk of, in addition to being unfair, affecting the relationship that is to be established. In other words, I have to be vigilant not to let myself be swayed by initial empathy. I need to be aware of the facts and remain objective.

To give an example of how complicated it is to rely on the subjectivity of first impressions, I will tell a joke that made me laugh but also led me to a deeper reflection:

A middle-aged lady decided to change dentists. People had spoken highly to her of a particular dentist, so she decided to consult with him. On the day of appointment, as she was driving over and thinking about the upcoming appointment, she thought his name sounded familiar. If it were who she thought it was, they would have studied together in the same school. Tall, blond, and charming, he had been very popular with the girls. She recalled him enthusiastically, starting to feel anxious about the upcoming appointment, remembering she had had quite a crush on him. She recalled, feeling romantic, the words of Chico Buarque de Holanda in one of his songs: "It is disconcerting to see a great love again."

Sitting in the waiting room, she could hardly wait to greet him. How would it be? She was finally attended by a bald man with a rather prominent belly, almost unrecognizable. Then she noticed his smile, which still carried a lot of the old joy of adolescence. She thus confirmed her suspicion that it was him. *Poor fellow*, she thought, *it's amazing how badly he has aged*. Smiling her best smile, she said coquettishly, "I think we've met; I was your contemporary at school."

He paused for a moment as if trying to match her to someone in his memory. He finally asked, "What subject did you teach?"

At first, I found this joke very good. Then it made me think. It seemed sad on second thought. Rarely do we find in the judgments we make about others the equivalent in terms of what we see in the mirror. We are much stricter with our neighbors than we are with ourselves. Putting myself in that lady's shoes, I thought I would probably have also been scared at how fast an old colleague had aged, without realizing I had also aged just as much or more.

It is astounding how quick we are to judge and how often we are wrong. We are alarmingly critical. We are eager to convince ourselves that we are better, more intelligent, more fortunate. As unusual as it may seem, I feel this falsely cheerful story taught me something. People probably look at me the same way I look at them. This realization humbled me.

It was exactly when I was reflecting on these issues of appearances and first impressions that I met Nicolas. Sitting at my desk, trying to be as fair as possible with the person in front of me, I heard one of the most fascinating stories I had yet heard. It turned out he was the descendant of royalty. Unintentionally, I caught myself looking for evidence of entitlement that I could not find. Apparently, I still had not rid myself of my prejudices.

Nicolas descended from Russians. Actually, to be more precise, he descended from Ukrainians. I learned that for several centuries the ruling dynasty in tsarist tradition had been the Kiev family, before the Romanovs, nobles who had been decimated by the 1917 Russian revolution. I did my homework and learned that the Kiev dynasty had been longer in power and had more remarkable leaders than the Romanov dynasty. For example, Ivan the Terrible had belonged to the Kiev dynasty. I was stunned to see the documents my young client showed me. They showed him to be a direct descendant of the tsars.

More than that, according to the rules of succession at the time, if the Kiev dynasty had remained in power until the present day, Nicolas would be the tsar of Russia!

At this exact point, my task was starting to take shape. If you were the admissions officer of a school and received an MBA application from someone who belonged to a tsarist dynasty would you not be interested in getting to know him better? I gambled on yes.

Upon hearing the personal story of that young man of royal blood, I realized he was born to be a winner, regardless of his ancestry. He had graduated first in his class, won a scholarship from his employer to get an MBA, and stood out in life for always being the youngest to reach positions of prominence in everything he set out to do. It was not difficult to predict that he would be offered admission by several schools.

His curriculum vitae was full of so many relevant examples of how he added value that we would not even have to evoke the past century of his family to get him in. We agreed, however, that we could not just overlook that which would make him unforgettable to anyone who read his application.

We thus decided to include in his application a timeline with the seven-hundred-year history of the leaders who came before him. On this chart, he highlighted the immense responsibility resting on his shoulders since he had been born, the onus of continuing to carry the flag of that remarkable family. The young Ukranian nobleman had grown up thinking that he was required to be successful, a load that is difficult for many to bear. For him, however, it served as a stimulus to overcome obstacles.

Out of the many schools where he was admitted, he chose MIT, where he also ended up being among the best students. Upon returning to the employer who had sponsored him, he quickly rose to the position of director, the youngest in the history of that bank. And I became a friend of a descendant of Ivan the Terrible.

24

The Parachutist

Augusto held an engineering degree from the University of Rio Grande do Sul and worked as a trader in an international bank in the city of Porto Alegre. His work history was good but relatively common. The number of engineers working in the financial market is very large, and the profession of trader is not among the most glamorous. A trader is the person responsible for negotiating the fees and prices of financial products marketed by the bank, usually by telephone, in one of those rooms that are equipped with high-tech Bloomberg and Reuters terminals, plus other gadgets that let traders monitor the progress of the market in real time.

A good trader has to be quick with numbers, good at communication, skillful at negotiating, and very perceptive. I have the image in my mind of professionals who work with a phone in each ear, in front of a screen full of numbers and graphs, and are able to process numerous information streams simultaneously, making large sums for the bank as effortlessly as if they were ordering a pizza from around the corner.

At day's end, the performance of these professionals is measured in the most straightforward way possible: by the profit they generate. Their pay also tends to be directly related to the profit produced, usually in the form of hefty bonuses that compensate for a low base salary. Thus, those who produce more, earn more. Good traders earn a lot of money. As a result, many of them do not feel motivated to study more, go to graduate school, or seek intellectual growth. In this career, people with high potential often end up settling in and doing the same job for years, without developing management skills and without ambition to rise in the hierarchy.

Definitely this was not the case with Augusto, an inquisitive and ambitious guy, concerned with self-development and highly motivated to find an MBA program abroad. His career had been marked by changes in areas and cities, always in search of professional growth—factors that are greatly valued by MBA schools, but in my view were insufficient to differentiate him from other good candidates with roots in the financial market.

Again, the solution came from a completely different context from the professional. On weekends, Augusto was devoted to a hobby that was quite different from his suit-and-tie routine: skydiving. He had even founded a school specializing in the Free-Fly skydiving style, where the goal of the practitioners was to open the parachutes as close to the ground as possible. It sounds risky, but according to Augusto, they are extremely careful and well-trained, and the risk of death in this activity is infinitely smaller than the risk of death from car accidents.

Upon hearing this story, I suggested to Augusto that he tell it in all his applications with the following introduction:

> Parachutist, in Brazilian slang, is a word that has a negative connotation, designating the individual who enters into a selection process ill-prepared and reliant on luck to reach his goal. Nothing could be further from the truth. Parachutists are obsessed with preparation, planning every detail before jumping. Everything is important in the preparation: their athletic conditioning, the weather, specific training, equipment. Nothing is left to chance, and every action is geared toward achieving the objective with the least possible risk.

From there, it was easy to show why he took his career as a trader so seriously. There was the same focus on challenge, the same careful and skillful search for the best way to achieve goals. In this context, Augusto managed to differentiate himself from most colleagues in the financial market, adding spice to his application. He was admitted to some of the top schools (Wharton, MIT, Columbia, Michigan, and Duke). By choosing Wharton, Augusto certainly leaped toward greater professional success.

25

The Man Who Dreamed of Wall Street

The radio alarm clock broke the silence in the room. Opening his eyes, already feeling worn, he prepared for another day like all the rest. He read the news before getting out of bed:

> NEW YORK—Stocks on Wall Street closed yesterday at a slight increase, thanks to good business results and despite the strong rise in oil prices. Completing four straight weeks of increased value today, the Dow Jones Industrial index rose 15.44 points (0.12%) to 13,120.94, its third consecutive record. Nasdaq advanced 2.75 points (0.11%) to 2,557.21, its highest level in six years.

He imagined himself on Wall Street, far away from where he was now; a place where he was feeling suffocated. Sighing, he threw the covers aside and stood up, carrying the world on his shoulders. At least that is my impression of how Artur was acting before he came to see me. My experience with him was most rewarding because I helped him change careers at a point in life when many people no longer have the courage to start over.

From an outsider's viewpoint, his career seemed well under way. Before the age of thirty, he had become the director of a medium-sized health insurance company, having had several entrepreneurial experiences first. One of these was the creation of the first software for vocational guidance in Brazil, acquired by many schools throughout the country. In addition, he had a restaurant in a business district that specialized in the lunch crowd. Beneath this veneer of accomplishment, however, Artur was unhappy, stressed, unmotivated, and underutilized, yearning for a radical change that would allow him to better exploit the potential that he knew he had. He dreamed of working on Wall Street, the Mecca of the financial markets, where he believed he could develop further than he had so far.

Having experienced a similar situation, I related to his suffering. At the time I worked as a doctor, nothing irritated me more than people around me minimizing my misgivings, saying that I had everything to be happy and therefore should not complain about what life offered me. However, things do not work that way. The yearnings of our souls have their reasons that rationality knows nothing about.

Analyzing Artur's trajectory, I noticed signs of intensity, an ongoing focus on growing, expanding horizons, and facing personal challenges. However, he constantly downplayed his achievements, being ever modest. For example, he assigned no importance to the fact that he had been the best student in his engineering course. In fact, he didn't even know; he only discovered this fact when he got his transcripts to send to the MBA programs!

One of Artur's insecurities regarding the MBA program and the journey we were beginning concerned his level of English, which was only intermediate at the time. He thought that, nearing thirty, he would have difficulty obtaining the scores needed to get into top schools. I showed him my own stats, instilling in him the idea that yes, it was possible for him to get into an MBA program if he dedicated himself to preparing for the TOEFL and GMAT exams. I also made him see that, contrary to what he believed, he had an interesting and compelling story. We just needed to tell it the right way, exploring and highlighting the positive aspects, such as his undeniable entrepreneurial spirit.

Through hard work and excellent time management, Artur balanced his tight schedule with his studying. As a result, he got excellent scores on the tests and was admitted to five first-rate MBA programs, including Wharton, the number one in the world for finance.

His transition continued effortlessly from there. He focused his MBA in the financial sector and, at the end of the course, was hired by a large US bank. Then he took up residence in New York and started working on Wall Street—just as he'd always dreamed.

I visited him once and was amazed at his standard of living. I could see the peaceful environment in which his children were growing up. Unlike most American executives who dream of living in Manhattan, paying exorbitant prices per square foot, he had chosen to live on Roosevelt Island, which sits right in front of Manhattan. He had one of the most stunning views of New York City for half the rent. It was a smart choice in my opinion.

After a few years, I had lunch with Artur during one of his visits to São Paulo and found that he was very happy professionally. Balanced, mature, and very well paid; he had completed a professional cycle and was in Brazil in a leading position in the financial market. Later, we met again at a Wharton event in Rio de Janeiro, where we celebrated the success of this radical change in his career, which came about relatively late in his professional development. He had demonstrated that it is never too late to dream bigger dreams.

26

The Ambassador

Fernando C. had great potential. It was evident from the first interview, where I noticed his acumen, good communication, interpersonal skills, friendliness, and the extremely rare quality of knowing how to listen. His academic background also impressed me. Without going to a prep school, he had come in seventh place among thousands of candidates in the competitive entrance exam to Fundação Getúlio Vargas—arguably, Brazil's premier business university, FGV is widely regarded as one of the country's top institutions of higher learning.

A year earlier, while still in high school, Fernando C. had already passed the entrance exam for FEA-USP, another highly competitive business school, even though he had done the exam only for practice. He confided to me his technique to overcome obstacles through a mind game he had created, in which he always tried to overestimate the challenges, trying to convince himself that he would not be able to meet them—that way, he never relaxed and was able to give his best until the goal was reached.

With the kind of attitude that initially gave me the erroneous impression of exaggerated modesty, Fernando C. led a life marked by great professional achievements. When it came time to do an internship, he was one of the golden boys, chosen among thousands of applicants to the program of the Banco Nacional—at the time, considered one of the best breeding grounds for young talent. There, he quickly made his mark, winning a leading position. His life seemed on track—that is, until he had a quite unexpected surprise.

His story made me think about how we are not always masters of our fate. No matter how good we may be at planning our futures, we are often placed in the middle of events we have not planned, events capable of changing happy trajectories that would have remained unchanged if it were only up to us. On a day like many others, early in the morning, Fernando C. was driving to work, feeling motivated as he always did. He arrived at his building to find a Unibanco banner covering the Banco Nacional logo. Nobody, not one of the employees, knew what had happened. It was another acquisition in the financial market, something that nowadays has become quite commonplace, but at that time took everyone by surprise.

Upon being invited to create an integration committee, whose mission would be to facilitate the transition of the staff, Fernando C. did not hesitate. He started to play a key role in the transition, using his leadership skills to help others in that difficult time. That is how he started working at Unibanco.

Eventually, he was nominated to receive a full scholarship to get an MBA abroad. Despite having an enviable vocabulary in Portuguese, the always pragmatic Fernando C. knew he would need to improve his English vocabulary in order to overcome the challenge that the GMAT represented.

With great determination, he studied intensively for many months. I was amused by the way he found to accelerate the acquisition of a good vocabulary—the work he sent me was mostly in English, with some words in Portuguese mixed in when he was unsure about the translation. Not knowing a few words was not going to stop him! In the end, he produced wonderful essays with powerful examples of his ability to overcome obstacles. Even the episode of the banner covering the Banco Nacional logo was narrated, painting a life story that certainly pleased the admissions officers of the best schools in the world. He was admitted to several programs, including Wharton, which had been his goal.

But Fernando C.'s story does not end here. At Wharton, he quickly became a leader among his peers, winning everyone over and helping in every way possible. An illustrative episode occurred when I accepted his repeated invitations to visit Wharton. Following his advice, I took the train from New York's Penn Station to Philadelphia, and got off at the 30th Street Station there. I was just ten minutes from Wharton.

Total travel time: one hour and ten minutes. I guess that is why they say that Philadelphians reach the rush-hour Broadway shows before New Yorkers. Jokes aside, this is priceless information for Brazilian candidates who do not realize how close these cities are to each other.

I was very well received by Fernando C., who met me at the train station. He was a true ambassador for the school. After a short walk, he showed me the campus, the classrooms, and the admissions office. Over the weekend, besides introducing me to people, he took me to see some of the Philadelphia sights, including a famous local theater that has a remarkable role in US history. This theater stood in front of my hotel, and on my last night in town, a large crowd had formed near the theater, attracted by a popular performance. I wanted to see the inside of the theater, but we did not have tickets and did not intend to attend the play, which was due to start in ten minutes. I had all but resigned myself to not seeing the theater from inside, but not Fernando C. With his smooth talk, in the middle of the mass of people coming to watch the show, he convinced the girl in the box office to let us in just to look. I was astounded when she dropped the chain, allowing us access.

The friendship we developed made me admire Fernando C. more and more. After his return to Brazil, we had many lunches, which allowed me to keep abreast of his career advancement at the bank. He is now an executive with many responsibilities and much influence in the strategic decisions of the bank. Furthermore, he is one of the Wharton interviewers in Brazil and has helped many talented candidates go to Wharton. He participates in the Wharton Alumni Club of Brazil and attended the World Forum in Rio de Janeiro. Every year he has sent me several clients, including the son of the bank's president, who is currently a PhD candidate in economics at Columbia University.

I am glad to have been able to help him. The biggest reward for those of us who help people reach their dreams is seeing the final result. Having contributed to Fernando C.'s development into a successful professional and an outstanding person in all that he does, I am led to respect and enjoy what I do all the more.

27

Head of the Derivatives Desk

Regina was the shy type, very petite, seemingly frightened by everything that was happening in her life. Her transcripts were stellar. She was a former student of the prestigious Dante Alighieri High School, where she had won numerous academic awards, and had graduated in engineering from the Polytechnic School of the University of São Paulo (Poli), a course in which there were very few women. Always focused on studies and work, she had started working in finance as a trainee and then transitioned into an investment banking position. With recognized good performance, she had been recently promoted to head of derivatives—one of the few women in the Brazilian market to hold this position; such was this male-dominated territory.

Used to being part of the minority since her days at Poli, Regina was unmoved by the achievement. She simply rolled up her sleeves and fulfilled her obligations as well as she could. She managed to win the trust of all those who worked with her. However, she ended up facing another barrier, one that was even more decisive in the financial market: the lack of an MBA on her résumé. Investigating the prerequisites necessary to get into a good MBA program abroad, Regina knew she would have great difficulty in reconciling the process of admission with her demanding new job as head of derivatives. She was also determined to get her MBA in the US since she knew that would afford her more professional opportunities going into the future. She was, therefore, justifiably anxious when she met with me for the first time.

I analyzed her case objectively and advised her to postpone the MBA for a year. She could thus prepare calmly for the TOEFL and GMAT tests without the pressure of time constraints. The following year, once the tests were done, we could prepare the applications, giving them the full time and attention they required.

And that is exactly what happened. I was very impressed with the excellent scores she got. When the time came the following year, we worked on the applications calmly, telling the interesting story of a woman who had overcome many barriers imposed by prejudice. In the end, we had a winner in every respect: a woman (hence, a minority in the business world), good academic performance, good scores on the tests, remarkable performance in the financial markets, and an important leadership position at a young age. Regina was admitted to seven of the top MBA programs, among them Wharton, Stanford, and MIT.

We now had to deal with a good problem. As so many others of my clients, we had the dilemma of choosing one school among many excellent options. I suggested she go visit the schools to decide. She took my advice. She crossed the US from end to end, went to classes, visited the campuses, talked with students and professors, and managed to reduce the choice to two schools: Stanford and Wharton. In the end, she decided on Wharton, having fallen for the Brazilians who would be her future colleagues. In fact, attending a barbecue Regina organized, where I came into contact with her future classmates (many of them clients of mine), I was impressed by the spirit of camaraderie and affection among them.

After attaining her MBA, Regina was hired by another bank, Itaú-Unibanco. Today, she is an important executive of the bank, well prepared to face any challenge in the financial markets.

28

The Best Medicine

Harvard University is already very old for an institution in the Americas, a distinguished lady born in 1636. She is proud of being the oldest institution for higher education in the United States. She inherited her name from her main donor, Pastor John Harvard of Charlestown, who left her his library and half of all his assets.

Today, she has about 13,000 undergraduates, 6,600 graduates, and 2,300 professors, and receives the most donations of any school in America.

Seven US presidents, among them John Adams, John Kennedy, and George W. Bush, have studied there, along with nearly seventy-five Nobel Prize recipients.

It is considered one of the best universities in the world, a recognition that was recently endorsed by the conservative British newspaper the *Financial Times*, which placed the Massachusetts institution alongside the University of Cambridge in England in terms of academic excellence. Most courses offered by Harvard, whether undergraduate or graduate, are among the best in the world, as is certainly the case with its MBA program.

It has the third-largest library in the world, and the first among the universities, with more than fifteen million books. It has the largest budget of all the schools for research and teaching. In 2005, a little over $57 billion came into the coffers of the institution. It is not easy to attend Harvard. Among all applicants in 2006, only 9.1 percent were admitted.

Those looking in films for images of the school should watch the movie *Love Story* from the 1960s. It was the last recording allowed on campus. *Legally Blonde, The Firm,* and *Good Will Hunting,* all films that featured Harvard, for example, were filmed on sets that imitated the university.

They say that to be admitted at the Harvard MBA program it is necessary to have a loaded gun; for example, a letter of recommendation from someone of high caliber or political prominence. I can say with certainty that this idea is just one of those urban legends, which combined with the degree of competitiveness in the selection process of the school, eventually crystallized into a truism.

At least it sounds like a good excuse for those who are not admitted there. I am a case in point. Harvard was the only school that rejected me out of the top ten to which I applied in the 1983–84 biennium. Nowadays, I can see that my profile was not ideal for the school. I was a much better fit with MIT, Stanford, and Wharton; but back then, it was a bitter pill to swallow.

Over the years, several clients of mine have been admitted to Harvard. A great majority of them had no loaded gun, only recommendation letters from their bosses, directors, or presidents of the company. Rare were those who had the support of some so-called celebrity. When that did happen, it was in a valid context. Some were from prominent families, others were not. With the experience I have today, I would never cast suspicion on the fairness of the selection process at Harvard. I rely on several examples that confirm my perception.

One of these examples is Carlos X. A *Carioca* (as people from Rio de Janeiro are called in Brazil) with an engineering degree, he had worked for years as a consultant for Accenture. He had excellent training and a great career. He also had good prospects for wealth, since his father was the owner of a midsize pharmaceutical company. He could look forward to assuming a leadership position at the company, succeeding his father. Crowning this, he had obtained excellent results on the GMAT and TOEFL.

Things seemed to get tougher when we trained for the interview. I worried about the stance that he insisted on taking, one of diverting attention from himself. Having grown up under the influence of an entrepreneur with a strong personality, Carlos X. became accustomed to saying little and not confronting people, conveying an image of shyness that cast a shadow on his great potential. Given that every year, Accenture has hundreds of consultants sending applications to the best

MBA courses, this kind of attitude could work against him. It would be a disadvantage in a tiebreaker with his peers, perhaps preventing him from achieving his objective.

As always, I suggested expanding his range of options. One of the alternatives was New York University, a center for excellence in finance, which asks for an essay quite different from the other schools. Its directive reads:

> *Describe yourself creatively to your colleagues. You can use*
> *photos, drawings, objects, texts, or any form of expression that*
> *is not electronic.*

This question has existed for many years. I have encouraged my clients to be as creative as possible to differentiate themselves from the competition. I suppose there must be some closet full of trinkets at NYU sent by my students.

In the case of Carlos X., we worked very hard to find an innovative way to display his qualities. We opted for a customized over-the-counter drug carton. His name would be used as the name of the medicine, and the leaflet would describe his characteristics as if they were ingredients in the drug (100 mg of Leadership, 99 mg of Motivation, and so forth). Using his father's laboratory, he managed to make the box so professional that it looked like a real medicine carton (I keep a copy of it in my office).

It is curious that, in principle, his father criticized the idea, saying it seemed like child's play, not a selective process for an MBA. However, we believed it to be a good idea and sent the box. When Carlos X. was admitted, I had to restrain myself not to call those who had criticized our plan. The Harvard application, in turn, did not give rise to such creative ideas (no medicine box there). However, we used many of the ideas that arose from the NYU application to answer questions asked by that more traditional school. We had our confidence heightened by the quality of the material produced so far. In addition, we trained for the interview quite a bit. In the end, the whole thing worked. Carlos X. got into Harvard and several other schools, opting to study at Harvard.

After graduation, he was hired by McKinsey and had an excellent career in that global consulting firm.

29

The Son of the Trumpeter

I have said little so far about how music was and still is important in my life. The seventies and eighties found me still very young. We heard a lot of bossa nova back then. Since I had a piano at home, I tried to learn to play it. I could fool people into thinking that I could play, and still can, with a repertoire including songs from Tom Jobim, Chico Buarque de Holanda, Vinicius de Moraes, Carlinhos Lira, and Nara Leao.

Our school group was more into Brazilian music than rock, another of the fads of the time. We knew the lyrics by heart; there was always a guitar and a stool around. Disposition and physical fitness to stay up all night playing were not a problem. Many romances started at that time, eye to eye, in the slow cadence and melodious sounds of those immortal songs, still played worldwide. The acoustic trio comprised of bass, keyboards, and drums, where extraordinary musicians could show their stuff, made our heads spin.

From that to jazz was a small switch, perhaps because of the similarity of many of the chords and the frequent use of improvisation. Soon our tastes got more sophisticated. The closing hours of our parties would find us frantically banging out the boogie-woogie, expressing with the tapping of our left hands the joy of being together. We eventually moved on to the more elaborate music of people like Dave Brubeck, Chick Corea, Thelonious Monk, Ella Fitzgerald, Louis Armstrong, and Billie Holiday. Right now, as I am writing, the delicious sounds of Miles Davis's trumpet invade my ears. What a genius.

Considering my passion for music, meeting Masao was a blessing, although it took some coaxing to find out his father was a gifted and accessible musician who often played in São Paulo. My meeting with Masao started with a brief introduction followed by a blunt question: "My story is not interesting—I studied engineering at the Polytechnic School of the University of São Paulo, specialized in mechatronics, then went to work at General Motors as an engineer. That's all. Could I be admitted to a top-ten with that story?"

Again I was hearing the old insecurities that I find in most of my clients. I interviewed Masao in search of details that could make a difference. As I got to know him, I came to admire the richness of his life story. His academic curriculum was impeccable and included a very interesting story about a robotics competition. His team had won the Brazilian competition and went to represent the country in the finals in Japan. His career at GM was ascending and increasingly directed toward management activities. Here, perhaps, was the reason for Masao's initial discomfort. For many engineers, management activities are considered less noble, seen more as bureaucracy than as something that adds value.

I go to great lengths to correct this distorted view common among most of the technicians I have met. I believe exactly the opposite. Management is the lifeblood of organizations; it is what makes things happen, distinguishing winning companies from losers.

That is how Alfred Sloan thought. He was the president of General Motors for decades. He established managerial policies that turned the company into the largest automobile manufacturer in the world. He bet on diversification, technological innovation, and internationalization to become larger than life. As a former MIT student, I always admired the history of this great strategist. Not only did he have a visionary's perspective, but he was a sponsor and enthusiastic supporter of our business school, which now bears his name (MIT Sloan School of Management).

With these thoughts in mind, I began to investigate details of Masao's personal life. Though he was puzzled by my interest in his extracurricular activities, he eagerly shared the details. I loved finding out, for example, that his father was a trumpeter and played at Bourbon Street, a great venue in São Paulo to hear good jazz. I could not resist. I gathered some friends and, on a Thursday evening, went to hear Masao's father play. I was surprised by the excellent quality of the band and performance of Masao's father, the group's trumpeter. A white-haired Japanese man with a very youthful face, he played in the best style of Louis Armstrong, singing occasional snippets with that typical, husky voice, very similar to the original artist. He was very nice; we talked a little about his son's plans to do an MBA course of studies. He fully supported the idea, despite the differences in style and career between them.

When Masao and I met again at the office, he told me about a book his father had helped write about the family. I borrowed it and quickly became delighted with the facts of the story. I was moved by the story of Masao's grandfather, the first Japanese student in history to be admitted to an American university at the turn of the nineteenth century. He had graduated from Columbia and been a great supporter of studies in the family.

With such elements as these, it became easy to "sell the sushi," as I like to joke, in Masao's case, telling the story along the lines of an unusual Japanese tale. Admitted to several of the top-ten schools, he chose Wharton. Later, when he changed careers to strategic consulting, he was admitted to one of the world's leading companies in this field, the Boston Consulting Group. He currently leads projects in Italy.

30

The Gladiator

I love strong, enduring stories. Everything David told me in our first meeting was, in my view, pure gold. I found myself almost instantly visualizing his application essays. With his life path full of interesting turns and dramatic twists, I looked forward to helping him outperform the competition.

However, throughout the period of preparation, it became clear that, with the time that we had, he would not achieve a very high GMAT score. Nor would his personal and professional tracks allow him to postpone the MBA until the next year. We decided instead to work extra hard on the essays, narrating the beautiful path of self-transcendence that he had taken, starting early on, when he needed to resist his parent's desires in order to follow his own destiny.

David grew up in the Bom Retiro neighborhood in São Paulo to parents of Jewish origin, owners of a small clothes factory like many others in the neighborhood. But there were differences between other families and his, which had come from Lebanon via London, where David was born and had learned early to speak English well. They were, so to speak, globalized compared to the many neighbors who had never left Bom Retiro.

A little background: The current district of Bom Retiro in São Paulo began to be occupied in the early nineteenth century. It was a region with both rural and urban characteristics. Since it was near the city center, it offered easy access to people who were heading there. Along with the Brás and Luz neighborhoods, it formed the first set of working-class communities in the capital. In 1880, with increased immigration from Europe, the neighborhood began to be more heavily urbanized, becoming characterized from the outset as a place full of immigrants and proletariats, thanks to the presence of various industries. Thus, it came into being as a manufacturing neighborhood. From its lowlands, emerged clay pottery as well as spinning and weaving factories. People lived amid the trade industries. Many Italians settled there.

The 1920s brought many Jewish families to the area. They settled primarily in the upper part of the neighborhood, closer to the railroad. Mostly Russian Jews fleeing the crumbling tsarist empire, they were traders, selling many different items on the streets of downtown São Paulo and in the neighborhoods where they lived. Later, Jews from Poland joined the Russians.

In the '30s, Bom Retiro became an increasingly Jewish region, although the Italians still predominated. By the early 1940s, however, the atmosphere was almost entirely Jewish: synagogues; Yiddish-speaking people; men with typical, long beards; and shops selling Jewish food. Only later, in the 1960s, with the arrival of Koreans, did the picture change. Nowadays, Bom Retiro is a neighborhood where diverse groups of people live together harmoniously, revealing a poignantly peaceful disposition. It is undoubtedly a place with a very inspiring story.

In the nineties, as a youngster working many years with his father in a garment factory in Bom Retiro, David felt a growing desire to follow a different path, live a different dream. While his father imagined his son running the family business, David yearned to get out and travel, see the world, grow intellectually. He found in his studies as an economics major support for his liberation. At university, he met other people and saw new realities. He began to do internships in companies that were very different from the world he had previously known. After his graduation, he did a specialization course in business administration at FGV, the renowned Brazilian business school.

He had an important experience at Cinemark. The company, innovators in the business of movie exhibition, entered Brazil with plans for accelerated growth, completely transforming the entertainment industry. By establishing new standards in the market, it eventually buried the old neighborhood cinemas. The first Brazilian Cinemark staff did not have experience in the field; they learned everything they knew by trial and error, simply rolling up their sleeves and getting to work. David made a career in this business, becoming Cinemark's operational and development manager, responsible for twelve multiplex theaters and more than seven hundred employees, thus moving in a very different direction from his brothers and cousins who were still in the garment ghetto of Bom Retiro.

Eventually David wanted to climb the next steps in his career, for which he clearly needed an MBA. When we first met, he was not aware that the difficulties he had faced in life (including financial difficulties), the conflicts with his father and brothers, his departure from the family business and neighborhood, and so many other events with strong dramatic content, could help him. I showed him that his tremendous ability to overcome obstacles would be very well regarded by the programs to which he aspired. That story fits perfectly with the American dream of the self-made man.

To illustrate his accomplishments, we used the creative question from the NYU application to compare him to the hero of the movie *Gladiator*, which was a huge success at the time and was being aired in Brazil by Cinemark. We set up a cardboard Gladiator with David's face, pointing out the similarities between his life and that of the character.

It worked. He was admitted to NYU and did his MBA there. However, in the first few weeks of living in New York City, even before classes began, David faced another problem worthy of a gladiator. He suffered a motorcycle accident and had to put both arms in a cast. I can only imagine that the beginning of his MBA was not hands-down easy.

None of this was enough to knock out the gladiator. Back in Brazil, he became involved in educational projects for some time, eventually resuming his career in the film industry. From being a PlayArt executive, he went on to become a director of Fox Films, and is now recognized as one of the behind-the-scenes stars of the entertainment industry in Brazil.

31

The Nerd Who Wasn't

Denis was one of those good students who looked like he was a good student. Not that I have anything against that, but we cannot deny that there is a pervasive prejudice against people who spend most of their time studying. I remember my time at Dante Alighieri High School, where I often earned medals for academic achievement. I was obliged to hear the same jokes over and over about being a nerd. It is only when we are older that we learn to appreciate the benefits of not being part of the crowd and become able to ignore the taunts.

MIT is a university that gained the reputation to be home to some of the world's greatest nerds: thick glasses, pocket protector, and a slide rule, distracted air, very high IQ, and assumed incompetence in dealing with the trivial matters of everyday life. But, to be clear, while these types occasionally appeared in the MIT schools of engineering, physics, and mathematics, they were not part of the business school, which is in a separate building and has nothing to do with that stereotype. Prejudice, however, existed, and would even hurt some business graduates when it was time to apply for a job.

I recall seeing a documentary made at MIT in which theater actors were hired to deliver a course for engineering students on being social. It was hysterically funny. The first task of the students of the course was deceptively simple: to cross a room carrying a book. The first who tried was clumsy and got a bit more than a look of disapproval from the actors. They made a huge fuss, crying out, "It's all wrong! You need to swing your arms, not press the book against your chest. You have to look at people, smile, look up from the floor, chin up, butt out!"

The student had to walk across the room twenty times in order to be considered suitable by the teacher-actors. Believe it or not, the course was for real and now is part of the engineering curriculum.

This story applied to Denis. Some data from his history could potentially generate bias in the selection process. The son of a college professor, he had become accustomed to speaking in a professorial manner, using a Portuguese that was too correct, probably reinforced by the first career he embraced: an auditor in a large consulting firm. Auditors face some prejudice, naturally, since they are trained not to establish relationships with people so they can perform their work in a cold, impartial, and objective manner. Some critics say that, for auditors, everyone is guilty until proven innocent.

Denis had graduated from FEA-USP, one of the most respected business programs in the country and part of the University of São Paulo. His position as first in his class reflected his dedication to his studies, something that had been instilled in him early on by his parents. Deepening our conversation, I realized that Denis was actually very skillful at interpersonal relations, having won important positions and having succeeded in changing careers within the company when he went from auditor to consultant. Given his excellent performance, his superiors had authorized the change, thus gaining a motivated and competent manager of strategic consulting projects.

What most caught my attention were Denis's hobbies. He was a talented card player, particularly of *truco*, a traditional Brazilian card game in which those outside have the distinct impression that all players are cheating shamelessly. It is probably evident from my description that I cannot play it, but the game is nevertheless a lot of fun. Denis was also an amateur drummer who loved to animate samba circles. He also had done plenty of international travel, including an exchange program in Scandinavia, and had a huge range of knowledge accumulated throughout an intellectually voracious life. He was actually a nice guy to talk to—intelligent and articulate. In an initial contact, however, in front of a stranger, the image he presented was closer to that of an aloof auditor than an amiable card player.

At one point, I told him about the MIT documentary I described in the beginning of the chapter. It seemed important to me to emphasize the importance given to a student's image. We also decided to focus on the evidence that he had a well-balanced profile, with due attention paid, of course, to his academic and professional achievements. Moreover, we simulated interviews and exchanged feedback, until I was confident about his performance. In the TOEFL and GMAT, as expected, he had no major difficulties. At the end of the process, he was admitted to several schools, choosing to study at Wharton.

Another interesting aspect that increased my admiration for Denis was the issue of funding. In order to get an MBA, he obtained a loan from Citibank, which guaranteed funds up to US$110,000, payable in fifteen years at subsidized interest rates. By my calculations, he would be paying about US$900 per month, a small amount compared to the long-term wage increase that the course would give him. Nonetheless, courage, self-confidence, and determination are required to face a loan of that figure, attributes that Denis demonstrated from the beginning.

But that's not all. A few months after he started his MBA, I received news that Denis had founded a drum band at Wharton. Along with several Brazilians in his class, he was demonstrating our cultural sense of rhythm to the foreigners!

After graduating, he managed to once again make a career change for the better, becoming a successful finance professional in a large brokerage firm. He also interviews for Wharton in Brazil. I have no doubt that the hours of study, the loan, the sacrifice, and our efforts to adjust his image to his personality were worthwhile. He learned to be flexible and to take the risks necessary to achieve his career-change objective.

32

The Metamorphosis

Ever since Daniel Goleman published his work on emotional intelligence, human resources professionals have honed their methods to assess this dimension in applicants with the same precision with which they have for decades assessed intellectual capacity. Today there is consensus that high IQ alone does not guarantee success in corporations, and does not translate necessarily into attributes such as leadership, management skills, ethics, communication, teamwork, motivation, empathy, negotiation capacity, ability to coach, and many other skills that are essential to the good performance of a manager. According to Goleman, the qualities above contribute more than 80 percent of the factors of professional success.

Everyone agrees, too, that a good IQ is a prerequisite in this equation; that is, it is a necessary factor, but not nearly enough. Nor can one evaluate a person just by measuring his or her intelligence. Techniques such as group dynamics and simulation games have been introduced with the objective of seeking to measure these other, emotive dimensions of personality.

I clearly remember the time when only intelligence was measured or, at most, the combination of brainpower and expertise. In Brazil, this was ultimately represented by the still-common college admission exam, the *vestibular*—endless tests, complex and enigmatic, designed to measure different shades of reasoning, both those related to quantitative skills and those related to verbal skills. Another example of this type of test is the GMAT, but it is only one factor considered in the MBA selection process.

At my first meeting with Fernando B. (who insisted on being called by his nickname, Fefê), it was clear to me that he had a high level of emotional intelligence, apparent not only through his good performance in our interview, but also through his personal and professional history. Everywhere he went, Fefê shone. Demonstrating strong leadership abilities since his schooldays, he had built as wide a network of contacts and friends in the most varied of social circles. He was a popular and well-liked guy; everyone wanted him around.

Fefê's choices during high school led him to devote himself diligently to the practice of tennis, becoming a champion in numerous tournaments and ranked among the best in his category. For a time, he seriously considered becoming a professional player, resulting in neglect of his studies as he devoted himself to his training sessions. Thus, at the time of the *vestibular*, he only gained admission to a business course at a night school with a second-tier reputation. Soon, however, he began working in the corporate world, acquired a taste for it, and abandoned the idea of professional sports.

In the workplace, Fefê continued to demonstrate his strong leadership skills and quickly achieved a managerial position. He devoted himself increasingly to his corporate career, and even less to his studies. He perpetuated the legend that he was not born to study, but to work. That way, when his employer nominated him to receive a full scholarship, planning to pay for his MBA abroad, he came to my office as if he had won a Trojan horse, a gift intended to trick or cause harm to the recipient. His initial reaction was of deep concern. He did not consider himself qualified to pass the GMAT, and he was afraid he would ruin the good image that he had built professionally, by not attaining admission at a strong MBA program.

The first practice tests we did showed that he was indeed lagging behind. In addition to being unprepared for such tests, Fefê was barely proficient in English and had difficulty with the TOEFL. The good thing was that we had a few months ahead of us and a lot of motivation. We could thus initiate the metamorphosis needed in Fefê's life. He told me later that he had never studied so much in his life as in all those months of preparation. At first, every time he sat down to do a practice test he would start sweating and become increasingly nervous. Gradually, however, he started improving his performance.

By the time of his GMAT tests, Fefê had reached a reasonable score on the practice sessions, although he was still about fifty points short of ideal. On the eve of the exam, his English teacher, Heloise, suggested he stop studying and do a session of Shiatsu for relaxation. He followed her advice.

I've often read about athletes who only give their best performance when the competition is for real. Something to do with adrenaline, motivation, challenge; I'm not sure, but the fact is that this was the case with Fefê. He got a 700 on the GMAT! It was an extraordinary score at the time, reached only by engineers with a lot of mileage on IQ tests (nowadays, with the proliferation of excellent test-prep centers, it is far more common to reach 700-plus on the GMAT). But this was what we needed. The result, combined with Fefê's excellent professional and personal histories, crowned by excellent interviews, eventually rewarded him with admission to several schools, Wharton among them.

More important than the goal attained—the chance to study at Wharton—was the remarkable amount of confidence that Fefê developed in his academic potential. The legend that he had mistakenly created about himself (that old lack of academic brilliance) could, in the long run, have been very damaging to him. Fortunately, it collapsed in a timely fashion, becoming nothing more than a myth.

What followed was predictable: absolute professional success, a rapid rise in the business world, leadership among Wharton alumni (he is also an interviewer), entrepreneurial initiatives, a happy marriage, and children. A well-balanced executive, successful in all spheres of life, Fefê is one of the friends that I hold close to my heart.

33

The Repentant Mafioso

For readers not familiar with the phrase in this title, the idea of the repentant Mafioso refers to a system used in the United States to combat the Mafia. In this system, informants, generally ex-mobsters who have decided to leave the world of crime, have their sentences reduced or forgiven in exchange for testifying against their former compatriots. In Italy, they would be the *pentiti* of the Clean Hands operation. Through this system, many families who once dominated the American organized crime scene were neutralized, as were corrupt politicians who had connections with the Mafia. Nowadays, the practice is common throughout the world, including Brazil.

I started to employ this term in the brainstorming sessions with clients who had neglected their studies for many years. I used it to refer to those who had retaken the noble path later in life, somehow managing to compensate for wasted years, either through work, additional courses, or international exchanges. In this context, I consider myself a repentant Mafioso! During medical school, I did not commit myself to studying as I should have. As I have said, I did not identify with that career, and so did not give its study my best effort. I was, however, able to enjoy an academic comeback through the MBA degree process.

Considering my own career trajectory, then, it is not surprising that I have particular empathy with clients whose cases are considered difficult. I believe it is never too late to build a better future. The MBA program in particular is helpful in that regard, aiding people with diverse types of academic training. These difficult cases are not so rare. I get many career-switchers, nearly a third of the total, showing that often our first vocational choices are wrong—perhaps because they occur too early in our lives.

Among the many *pentiti* I have helped, I highlight the extreme case of Sergio, another *Carioca,* who for most of his life had preferred surfing to studying. Slow to engage in academics, he eventually studied economics in a college not among the best in Rio de Janeiro. When he came to me he was around thirty years of age and would graduate only at the end of that year.

Sergio's life, however, was very interesting. Professionally, he demonstrated entrepreneurial capacity, having done well in the cosmetics industry. Personally, besides being a sportsman, he had traveled the world and could communicate well in English, although he needed to polish his grammar. Our biggest question mark was the math section in the GMAT, coupled with the novelty of submitting his applications before the date of his university graduation. I had yet to see that circumstance, and wondered how this quirk would be received by the schools to which he applied. Most good MBA programs require at least two years of professional experience after college.

My diagnosis: He would need a great GMAT result, and his grades in the last semester would have to be fantastic in order to convince admissions officers that his experience could make up for the academic issue. Additionally, his work life, even though it took place *during* his college years, would have to be considered in full. Finally, once he graduated in November, he would have to convince his university to issue his transcripts with unusual urgency, sending them out to the various MBA programs in a sufficiently timely fashion.

Aiming to explain the belated graduation, we used the analogy of repentant Mafioso. We showed that his studies had never been a priority in his life, that he had gone to night school, and that he had stretched out his curriculum in the early years, aiming not to disrupt his career, which had been developing very well. By contrast, we demonstrated, in his final semester, that he had *repented*, focused more on his studies and obtained good grades, thus supporting our argument with evidence.

As planned and agreed, Sergio in fact did study hard, getting both top marks in his last semester and a good score in the GMAT, nearing 700. The Brazilian university cooperated and released the transcript in early December, certifying his graduation before the rest of the class's official transcripts were issued.

His efforts paid off. He was admitted to several highly ranked schools and chose to attend Duke. Upon completion of the course, he got a great job in Chicago and now lives there. His wife has just been admitted to the MBA program at Notre Dame. I could say that the couple has taken full advantage of the second chance that studying brought about in their lives!

34

The Paradigm Breaker

Among the many legends surrounding the selection process at Harvard, perhaps the most entrenched of all is that once rejected, a candidate will never have a chance of being admitted. However, my client Priscilla exploded this myth.

The first time Priscilla came to my office, she began to cry almost as soon as she sat down. With tears streaming down her cheeks, she explained that she had always dreamed of studying at Harvard but had been rejected the year before. She believed that she didn't stand a chance as a reapplicant.

Her academic and professional achievements were impressive. She had graduated from ESPM (Escola Superior de Propaganda e Marketing) and had an interesting career in marketing, working in a multinational company that manufactured cleaning products. She was also involved with community activities and had great depth of character.

Her writing showed a unique style, sensitive and profound at the same time, which pleased me greatly. It was, however, very different from the straightforward manner used by most engineers and administrators who seek an MBA. Also, her GMAT was not very high. I believe that the combination of these factors had resulted in her failure on the first try.

Upon further exploration, I found out about professional achievements of hers that had not been showcased in her earlier application. One of them—in my opinion, the most striking—had been omitted because of advice she'd received from a consultant concerning the following circumstances:

One of the main products of the company she worked for was a toilet cleaner, a competitor of the then market leader, Pinho Sol. Priscilla was responsible for developing the product marketing campaign with the help of a leading advertising agency. One of the ideas that had been approved and implemented in the campaign used billboards scattered throughout the great avenues of major Brazilian cities. In them, a toilet containing a three-dimensional field of wildflowers jutted out of the billboard. Sales soared after the campaign was launched. Later that year, the product exceeded the sales of the competitor, replacing it as market leader.

I thought it was a great story, but in her application, the story had been stripped of its important details—most notably the toilet—rendering it diluted and flat. Without a full explanation, the achievement had lost its appeal. The prior consultant's argument, which I disagreed with from the start, was based on prejudice against a subject that was not very "noble"—the toilet. However, success makes no distinction. I've seen success crown people who worked with waste processing, condoms, alcohol, and even firearm sales. Why not a toilet cleaner?

I advised her to go ahead with the reapplication to Harvard and to try a few more schools. Priscilla studied hard and got a better score on the GMAT (she reached a 700), a resounding achievement, given her inclination toward humanities. She redesigned her résumé to be more objective, and told in detail the story of the toilet cleaner. We also emphasized the community work that she had been involved with since her schooldays and her power of influence over executives in the company, demanding and achieving improvements in the cafeteria and in labor conditions. In short, instead of trying to hide her sensitive side, we demonstrated the positive results that this had brought her.

To our delight, she was admitted at several MBA programs, including Harvard. We had managed to break the paradigm that reapplicants are not admitted at Harvard, and also demonstrated that there is room for sensitive people there, despite what some people say.

After finishing her MBA, Priscilla got an excellent job in the United States, where she lived until recently. Her case was an example to her younger brother, Julio, who was also my client, and who repeated his sister's feat by going to Harvard as well.

35

The Shinto Monk

Unlike my mother, a devout Catholic, I am not religious. I have the credentials but do not follow the rules. In fact, I have very particular views on religion. I believe in the psychological importance it plays in comforting humans in times of crisis, providing answers to existential questions that have afflicted us from time immemorial, and above all, exercising an unquestionable role of social benefit by disseminating the principles of good conduct and helping people in need or who have strayed from an honorable path. On the other hand, I always shocked my mother by saying that God is the most wonderful creation of man, no matter what religion in question.

Issues concerning faith, of course, are quite delicate subjects for an application. Biases may occur. For example, would a Muslim candidate be evaluated impartially by an admissions officer if that officer had happened to lose a loved one in the tragedy of September eleventh? There is no way of knowing. Given potential pitfalls such as these, I try to steer clients away from the subject, unless religious involvement has great relevance to the candidate's life and application. Even so, I advise my clients always to emphasize the social side of belief, the contribution to the community arising from this involvement, as opposed to the dogmas.

Suga was a Japanese Brazilian client who taught me something about Shinto, though he also was not an expert. We researched it together and found that it is a religion highly geared to the practical aspects of people's lives. Just like Buddhism, it emphasizes harmony between humans and the nature surrounding them, with emphasis on daily seeking to solve the trivial problems that plague communities.

In general, Shinto is practiced in temples, where the faithful look for objective solutions to their problems, seeking advice from religious leaders on issues of health, housing, personal finances, marriage, and other universal concerns. These leaders are wise people capable of dispensing good advice. They live in temples, dress like monks, and devote themselves full time to their work.

Suga's connection to Shinto happened almost by chance, coming to help us in the application process like a blessing from God. He was one of several candidates who had been offered sponsorship by his employer. His life history, however, had few anecdotes to help spice up his application. A hardworking guy who had always prioritized work and study over leisure and extracurricular activities, with little international experience, Suga was not exactly the ideal candidate for top business schools. I used to joke that his activities had no sex appeal—until one day he showed up with pretty dramatic news.

He had received an invitation from Japan to assume leadership of a Shinto temple in the hometown of his ancestors. By the rules of succession in the ancient temple, his uncle would be the next monk. However, the uncle was ill and had only daughters—who were not eligible by reason of their gender—and Suga's father, who might have been appointed in his brother's place, was now deceased. The search for successors led to my client, who was officially invited to be the new head monk. I was amazed when I saw the invitation in Japanese and an accompanying translation in English. It was obviously no joking matter.

As leader of the temple, our hero, until then an engineer with no monastic vocation, who had made his career working in human resources at Banco Itaú, would have to resolve all the practical problems of the inhabitants of a village in Japan. There, the majority of people had no access to hospitals, schools, banks, or other institutions of the contemporary world, counting only on the Shinto institution as a source of wisdom and advice.

After reflecting at length on the subject, we concluded that Suga should refuse the invitation, because his life had followed a different direction and not prepared him for such service to an unknown and foreign community. Nor were his career goals exactly in line with being a Shinto monk. However, given the importance of the matter, we decided the refusal should be communicated in person, and so we planned his trip to Japan. It ended up being an extremely compelling rite of passage. He met relatives he had not known about, visited the graves of his ancestors, and learned a lot about Shinto. He came to admire the simple lifestyle that the community had maintained for centuries.

Suga's refusal of this honorable invitation was understood, and another relative was selected for the task. For his part though, Suga brought back an inarguably unique experience, which he narrated in his application, following my advice. Combined with his good track record and good work performance, and supported by his employer's interest in sponsoring him, he ended up presenting a very interesting package, but now with much more sex appeal. It earned him admission to several schools, including MIT.

Even today, when I remember that story, I imagine the officers at MIT commenting on the application of the quasi-Shinto monk. Even if this fact did not make him a better candidate, it must have impressed on them the indelible memory that it impressed on me. It is usually the kind of thing that makes all the difference when it comes to outperforming the competition.

All of this happened a decade ago. Years later, to my delight, I received an invitation from Suga to attend an HR award ceremony. Seeing him onstage receiving the award for the project he led at Banco Itaú after completing his MBA at MIT, I confess that I was thrilled. And who knows? Maybe his Shinto heritage actually helped him win this award.

36

The Comeback

I love the music of Paulo Vanzolini, above all for its excellence. It is the perfect end-of-evening or end-of-relationship music. I also love old-school samba, especially Chico Buarque's recordings. Another gem is "Volta Por Cima" (Comeback), whose chorus—"get up, shake the dust off and make a comeback"—was eventually incorporated into Brazilians' everyday language, so commonly quoted now that most Brazilians probably could not tell you the origin.

Besides composing hits like "Volta Por Cima," Vanzolini had a rich life. He worked in radio and television, at the Museum of Zoology, and taught at the famous Colégio Bandeirantes. He graduated in zoology in 1947, married the following year, and went to the United States, where he obtained his doctorate in zoology at Harvard University. In addition to being a zoologist and devoted musician, he was Director of the Faculty of Animal Science at USP for many years and is considered an important scientist and renowned researcher in this field. I always admired his versatility, eclecticism, musical talent, and creativity.

I draw special attention to Vanzolini also because he was one of the founders of the Medicine Show, of which I was an active collaborator. I participated in the music and comedy shows—directed and staged by the students themselves—and I proudly included this involvement in my applications.

When I met Luiz Felipe, he was quite young, recently graduated from university, extremely thin with wild, curly hair reminiscent of the singer Caetano Veloso. His story reminded me of Vanzolini's chorus because he certainly made a comeback. From Goias, a state in the middle of Brazil, he was soft-spoken, with a slight accent softened from years of living in São Paulo. Luiz Felipe was laid-back and self-confident. He worked in a trading company that was owned by his extended family and that he had helped develop. The company's main product was new tires for trucks and buses, which they imported with exclusive rights from Japan. In his spare time, he practiced horseback riding, a sport he was passionate about.

I'll make a parenthesis to mention that the family business where Luiz Felipe worked was part of a very large and diversified group, with companies in the financial, transportation, and real estate sectors. The group is among the hundred biggest conglomerates in Brazil. Since college, he had been led to expect to develop a career in the family's companies. One day, however, things changed. The shareholders decided to professionalize the companies and established that no family member could be an employee. The relatives who worked in the business would be dismissed.

The news came during the preparation of his applications and took us by surprise, because the main theme of his essays was his future within the family business. We had to rethink not only the essays but his whole career plan. Among the areas that aroused Luiz Felipe's interest was consultancy, one of the fields most frequently explored by MBA students. Other areas that were appealing to him were marketing, finance, and entrepreneurship. He would have to expand his general knowledge in the field of management to keep these various options open.

We decided together to report the whole story as it had happened, including the loss of employment. We were clear in explaining that the dismissal had happened despite the great work he had done. Adding his good performances on the GMAT and at university, his passion for horses, and his international travel experience, Luiz Felipe presented a very competitive package. The end result was his admission to various top MBAs. He opted for the number-one school at the time, Kellogg, which is still recognized as one of the best in the world.

From the MBA at Kellogg to a successful career was a natural sequence. He worked for several years as a consultant in one of the largest global consultancies in the world, Booz Allen. Later, he was promoted to a management area, handling strategic segments of the company in Brazil. His successful career switch could, without a doubt, be considered a great comeback.

More than ten years have passed since that first encounter with Luiz Felipe, who has since matured into a successful executive. After I arrived in Lucca to write this book, I was speaking with my wife in São Paulo when I received with great pleasure the news that I consider his ultimate comeback. Luiz Felipe decided to leave consulting and devote himself entirely to a fashion business where he had already been a partner for three years, but which had been managed until then by his wife, Daniela, and her sister, Cris Barros, the Brazilian stylist and designer who founded the company.

The business evolved very quickly. They already have an outstanding performance in the Brazilian market and are exporting to various countries. With the experience accumulated throughout his professional career, I'm sure that Luiz Felipe will emerge as a successful entrepreneur in this industry, fulfilling the prophecy to which this chapter refers.

37

The Noble Frenchman

I often say about my work that I've seen everything, even people with more than a dozen last names—like Bernard. A direct descendant of French noblemen, he had kept all the last names in the family tradition, resulting in a mile-long name he was proud to know by heart. This fact just illustrated the very interesting life story of a man who came to me very young, having recently graduated in engineering and gone to work in telecommunications technology.

Although his career had been developing well, Bernard had realized that he would not enjoy working in a technical position forever. He wanted to explore his managerial side, travel, study abroad, seek international experience. I soon realized he had great entrepreneurial talent. He also showed strong desire to develop leadership skills, something he had not had the chance to do in the technical tasks assigned to him in the multinational company, of Scandinavian origin, where he had been working as an engineer.

As happens so often, he was strongly influenced by the example set by his father, who had gotten his MBA at Wharton and become the successful CEO of one of the major food companies in the world. As is often the case, his father, a very demanding person, wanted to see his son enrolled in a top-five MBA program.

Bernard had received an education that was 100 percent French. He had attended a French high school in Brazil and was so fluent in French that his English had been neglected. For a long time, perhaps due to a certain prejudice against English (which I believe is not uncommon among the French), he had not prioritized the language. He was capable of communicating in English, having travelled internationally for work, but had not developed the basic grammar needed to do well on the GMAT.

I remember having suggested he postpone his project for a year in order to study properly, especially considering that he was quite young. My advice fell on deaf ears. He was determined to handle the challenge that year so he could start his career switch as soon as possible.

From the personal point of view, his stories were interesting, permeated by much aristocratic international travel, sports, and education, as we joked during the brainstorming sessions, referring to the refined way he spoke, his table manners, and notions of etiquette at social gatherings.

Our challenges were substantial: young age and little experience, a highly technical career, and a below-average GMAT. I suggested we increase the number of schools he was applying to in order to increase his chances of admission. We decided to include Babson College, considered in all the relevant rankings to be the world's best in the area of entrepreneurship. The strategy worked and Bernard was admitted.

Our next obstacle was Bernard's father. We had to convince him that the course was good and would help change the direction of Bernard's career.

Aiming to accommodate the busy CEO's schedule, we agreed to meet at my office on a Sunday morning. It was not easy to convince this extremely assertive man who was obviously very accustomed to making important decisions. Babson was not among the names he knew. I showed him the rankings, discussed the program and its good reputation for entrepreneurship, and told him about several clients of mine who had gone to Babson and had been able to reach all their goals through the program. We talked all morning, did additional research on the Internet together, and by the end of the meeting, Bernard had won his father's support. Bernard would go to Babson.

As expected, he had a great MBA experience. He managed to give his career a new direction, getting an excellent job in one of the largest consulting companies in the world. Nowadays, he lives and works in New York City. I found it funny when I recently received an e-mail from him with only five letters in the address, making me think of his several surnames and the weight he had carried by having all those names to live up to.

38

The Man Who Navigated the Internet Bubble

It is common knowledge that it is more important to know when to get out of the stock market than when to get in. We should perhaps extend this understanding to human relationships. Who doesn't know couples who remain united only through inertia, long after the love has gone? Or someone who works in the same company for decades, not liking the job, but not doing anything about it?

During the Internet bubble, there was a real collective catharsis. People believed that, to get rich, all they needed to do was have a good idea and open a business on the Internet. The few analysts who warned people about the dangers of the bubble were labeled as pessimistic, backward, not in tune with the times, unable to understand the boldness of business that was sweeping the planet.

Cristiano joined the bandwagon. Originating from a family of entrepreneurs in the Brazilian state of Goias, he wanted to prove himself by opening his own business, regardless of existing opportunities within the conglomerate founded by his grandfather, an eminent political and economic figure in Goias. It is because of Cristiano that one of the first Internet service providers (ISPs) came onto the scene in that state, accompanied by a large number of pioneers who helped the industry to grow quickly.

During this gold rush, the figures were impressive and the deadlines tight. In the minds of those young web prospectors, long-term planning meant to value the company six months into the future—one year at most—and, based on these calculations, attract capital from investors. The ultimate goal was to become overnight millionaires. Some months before the bubble burst, there were already some signs of the end of the euphoria, but few people were willing to acknowledge those signs. The mood was more hysterical than rational.

At that point, Cristiano's company had grown enough that he started to lead meetings with other Internet providers to renegotiate contracts with investors. Heeding the signs of the cooling off, he sold his share of the business, managing to preserve much of his capital and getting out of the market before the bubble burst completely. Everyone knows what happened next. Bankruptcies, broken dreams, wasted resources, and the inevitable reality check that frustrated thousands of new businesspeople.

In my opinion, Cristiano's extraordinary capacity for market analysis and his courage in taking the appropriate action were enough to grant him admission to excellent schools. Yet he also had community involvement on his résumé. Put together, this made his application well balanced and complete. At the end of the process, he was admitted to the Stephen M. Ross School of Business at the University of Michigan.

When he returned to Brazil, coincidentally, we ran into each other at the São Paulo airport. He was with his father, president of the family conglomerate. Both reported with enthusiasm Cristiano's experience in Ann Arbor. He introduced me to his father saying that I was the consultant who had helped him get into Michigan. I quickly corrected him, explaining that he had gotten himself into Michigan with his initiative and, above all, his courage and knowledge of when to step back.

39

A Once-in-a-Lifetime Opportunity

The *Antonio Houaiss Dictionary of the Portuguese Language* is not very generous with the word *stereotype*. It defines it as follows: "something that describes a fixed or general standard, formed by preconceived ideas and fueled by the lack of real knowledge about the subject concerned." It is a description that is very close to the definition of *prejudice*.

In this sense, I always considered as unreasonable assertions that are very common in sports, for example that Caucasians are good swimmers, Africans are excellent sprinters, and that Asians are the best at martial arts. There is, as we know, no scientific basis for these statements. Based on these assumptions, we should also make statements like Brazilians are good at soccer, the English are very formal, the French are good lovers, and Italians are noisy. And all of this is without mentioning much more serious misconceptions, some of them quite offensive, which emerge from the imagination of many narrow-minded people.

There is no denying, however, that some racial stereotypes are universal. In the Western Hemisphere, at any latitude, Asian people are considered shy and withdrawn, focused only on study and work. Even though we know, rationally speaking, that once again we are using stereotypes, we nevertheless often apply such ethnic labels. I've seen people using this stereotype to justify the success of China's economy in modern times or, worse, trying to explain the West's failure in this regard.

Cris was a person who contradicted stereotypes. The daughter of a Chinese family from Taiwan, she had been raised in Brazil, incorporating Brazilian culture and values from an early age, but continuing to speak

Chinese at home with her family. She was extremely outgoing, talkative, cheerful, very friendly, as well as insightful and intelligent. She was far from the common stereotype of Asians.

Looking strictly at the academic and professional side, however, Cris certainly fit the mold. With good training, she had engaged in a career related to computers and data processing, winning good jobs, attending two colleges, and finally finding her place in the sun as a result of a lot of determination and personal effort. But she wanted much more and came to me thinking of getting her MBA.

Again, I encountered the recurring problem that a profile very focused on technical areas is not much appreciated by admissions officers, who generally seek evidence of leadership potential and management skills, and don't readily see these attributes in candidates from technical fields.

Cris herself did not consider that she had the requisite characteristics. Upon interviewing her, however, I realized she was wrong. Several technical tasks had led her to informal positions of leadership, although the title of the position and job function did not convey that. She had, for example, led an important effort to implement a product in Unibanco Bank. The project required technical knowledge and involved the ability to coordinate teams. It was common for her bosses, knowing her interpersonal skills, to ask her to lead such assignments. These endeavors generated rich material for her applications, so long as they were described from an appropriate perspective.

We took care to show how she was different from the "all-work" Asian stereotype, emphasizing her extracurricular activities and hobbies. When we finished, we had a good package, which earned her admission to UCLA, a great university in California. However, Cris's dream was to go to MIT. Everything indicated that, unfortunately, this objective would not be reached. Cris had rented a flat in Los Angeles and was already unpacked and ready to start classes at UCLA when the director of admissions at MIT called her in late August, two weeks before the start of school, asking if there was still time to accept an offer of admission. This required a radical change of plans and a lot of work to undo her apartment and move to Boston. Yet without hesitation, she answered straightaway, "Of course!"

To summarize the story, Cris graduated from MIT and earned the academic status she sought. She also became very active in the MIT alumni community, participating in events and information sessions, cultivating friendships, and expanding her network to professional levels undreamed of when it all started over ten years ago.

Cris has become a good friend. We often joke about the change at the last minute, calling it a once-in-a-lifetime opportunity. Although it required courage and daring, it brought her benefits that have marked the rest of her career. After working in important companies and taking entrepreneurial initiatives, she now works at Microsoft, where she provides consulting services to large corporations.

40

The Six-a-Side Soccer Guy

One of the themes that I like to explore with my clients is family history. As much as we try to differentiate ourselves from siblings or parents throughout our lives, we invariably find within our families someone who has served as a role model, influencing our personality.

Dennis had (still has, in fact) his grandfather as an example. A self-made man with great entrepreneurial spirit and a vocation for leadership, he inspired his grandson from early on.

As a teenager, Dennis was part of a group that met occasionally to play six-a-side soccer in a local court. Noticing the disorganization and lack of leadership in the group, he took the initiative to create an infrastructure that would guarantee regular rental income for the court. He also collected money to create uniforms, provide balls, hire a referee, and buy snacks and sodas, thus lending a much more systematic air to the matches.

Soon the group was as organized as a professional club. Dennis played regularly every week for years. In the style of his grandfather, he had become the club boss, respected for his leadership even by his older peers, despite his young age.

This simple story was used to exemplify the candidate's vocation as a leader, spicing up a story that had some positive aspects but was not distinctive. An engineer from an average school, with good grades, he had developed a respectable professional career working in well-regarded companies. When he applied for the MBA program, he was working as a financial analyst at Alcatel, a French telecommunications company, in a function that did not allow him to clearly demonstrate his managerial skills.

Once again, the NYU application helped us with its famous requirement that candidates describe themselves in creative, innovative ways. We had a friend of his who was a professional caricaturist draw up a caricature of him, adding various accessories symbolizing different aspects of his personality and activities: a laptop, soccer ball, phone, surfboard, and globe.

We added captions to each of the accessories, explaining their importance in Dennis's life. The finishing touch was the signature of the artist, and the caption that the drawing had been done for free by a professional, symbolizing Dennis's ability to cultivate a wide circle of friends, or, in business jargon, to network.

He ended up being admitted to NYU, where he was a great student, later getting a good job in the financial arm of a major Dutch group, the clothing retailer C&A. Interestingly, the company has been managed successfully for 160 years by members of the same family. Dennis was chosen to join a select leadership-development program with twenty people from several countries where the company does business. The program has as its aim to prepare these twenty high-potential employees to participate in the senior management of the company, an unprecedented move for the venerable group, and a high honor for Dennis.

Dennis's professional success largely mirrors his grandfather's, and I have no doubt that he will reach all the ambitious goals he decides to pursue. Dennis is driven by the healthy ambition to grow through hard work and continuous learning, a formula that I have never seen fail.

41

The Flight of the Seagull

To speak of Flavia, I have to deal with the theme of stereotypes again. I admit to not being politically correct in what I am about to say, but I am honest to a fault. When this gorgeous blonde from Rio de Janeiro, with the proportions typical of a runway model, came to my office, I imagined that her intellect could not possibly be as well developed as her looks. Once more, I was misled by a stereotype. She had been an excellent student her whole life, winning several academic awards and graduating in economics from Pontifícia Universidade Católica do Rio de Janeiro with high marks.

As a Paulista (someone from São Paulo), I know well that many people in São Paulo are unaware of the excellence of PUC-Rio in economics. Having lived two years abroad, I knew that the course is well recognized in other countries. Several Brazilian leaders and prominent economists have studied at PUC-Rio, and the college is widely recognized in American academic circles, more so even than some other schools in São Paulo.

Flavia, however, had some problems with self-esteem. During her adolescence, she had grown rapidly and become very tall. She considered herself awkward and was very shy. Since she was a good student, she got teased by her classmates. She had to learn to deal with relationship conflicts early on, differentiating herself through good performance. She was motivated by the dream of flying higher, meeting interesting people, traveling around the world, finally meeting the potential that had been constantly repressed in her. She loved to listen to the stories her father told. An airline pilot, he would tell her of the trips he made, often equating flying with the feeling of being on top of the world.

Flavia did a great job preparing for the GMAT. She obtained a score well above the barrier of 700 points. Professionally speaking, she had been developing well in the financial area. However, despite having a good story, she was still inexperienced, especially when it came to managerial activities. We needed to make her shine in order to draw the attention of the admissions officers and convince them to invest in her potential.

During brainstorming sessions we came up with the idea of creating an analogy of her trajectory with that of Jonathan Livingston Seagull, a little book that was very successful all around the world when I was a teenager. It told the story of a seagull rejected by the other seagulls because he flew better and higher. His biggest concern was to improve his ability to fly, while the others lived only for foraging. Bingo! It was the same story Flavia had lived. (I even ended up calling her Flavia Seagull.) The strategy worked. She was admitted to several top-ten schools, opting for Wharton out of all of them.

We ran into each other at the Wharton reunion at the Copacabana Palace in 2006. I was very happy with what I heard: after she got her MBA, despite still being very young, Flavia had managed to get a job in the area she wanted (finance) in her beloved hometown of Rio de Janeiro. To my delight, she had achieved all her dreams. It was a flight worthy of Jonathan Livingston Seagull. As Richard Bach, the author of that book, said, "The gull sees farthest who flies highest."

42

The Video game Girl

I remember with nostalgia the day I presented our son with his first video game. One of the first models in Brazil, it came with the *Ghostbusters* game. The tune, which echoed through all the rooms in the house, became implanted in my brain forever. The game was innocent, a basically linear route with a few variations and commands that did not require great skills from the players. It was a pleasant pastime that brought me many hours of socializing with my children. There is no denying that I witnessed the awakening of the video game generation, even if I was just a passerby.

Technology has, of course, progressed substantially since then. First, they launched the *Formula 1* video game, which I could still keep up with. Next came *Mario Bros.*, at which point I fell behind, as I did with soccer games, adventure racing, and the odious martial arts, full of bloodshed and special effects that became more realistic with each new version. With time, I stopped playing because of my absolute inability to compete with younger people.

The video game industry has become a fever that has swept the world, generating billions of dollars in revenue and finding in children and youth the most profitable market. It divides people automatically into two universes: players and nonplayers. A nonplayer like me would not dare, for example, to design a marketing and sales strategy for that type of product. Unaware of the attributes and competitive advantages of the segment, I would probably fail through ignorance of the fundamentals of communicating to that market. At least this was what I believed before being forced to revise my ideas.

My stereotype of the ideal marketing professional for video games was ripped to shreds when I met Juliana. A pretty, charismatic young woman, she had bright blue eyes that conveyed sincerity and captured the attention of the listener. She expressed herself well, her Portuguese polished by the best schools in São Paulo. She showed maturity and stability, despite her young age.

Juliana claimed she had been born to be a marketing professional, despite her father wanting her to be an engineer. She had gotten her marketing degree at ESPM (Escola Superior de Propaganda e Marketing), known for producing the best publicists in Brazil, and came shining through wherever she went. She had done internships in first-rate companies, having been admitted through competitive processes, always triumphing over thousands of candidates. She had learned to create campaigns for various products, from condoms to video games. At *Editora Abril*, the famous Brazilian magazine publishing house, for example, while still as an intern, she had persuaded her bosses to approve the mass distribution of condoms to accompany the popular Brazilian general news magazine *Veja*, within the scope of a campaign for the prevention of AIDS—a campaign that ended up being a great success.

When she first came to me, Juliana worked with Nintendo products, specifically the sort of modern, sophisticated games that had long since passed me by. During a conversation one day, I mentioned my theory about players and nonplayers. She convinced me I was wrong. She made me see that a good marketer can distinguish the important attributes of a product without deep prior knowledge about it. That is, the skills of marketing are universal and can be applied to different industries or products with minor adjustments.

Marketing can be defined as "the set of strategies and actions that provide the development, launch, and support for a product or service." Common understanding of marketing goes beyond this, however, and involves the development of a long-term, satisfying relationship between product or service and consumer; that is, the creation of a win-win situation. Marketing, of course, is not restricted to consumer goods, since it is also used to sell ideas, people (metaphorically speaking), and even social projects. Marketing techniques are widely applied in political systems and in different aspects of life.

My discussions with Juliana, while enlightening and instructive for me, also served as the basis for her essays, which easily demonstrated her versatility and ability to assimilate new knowledge. To complete the positive package, she got a great GMAT score (in the 700 range), which, together with her excellent academic performance in college, increased her chances of admission. And indeed, she achieved it, gaining offers of admission to several famous schools, including Kellogg, her first choice. Nowadays, she is a marketing executive for Johnson & Johnson. I am not sure which products are under her responsibility, but I'm sure they're in good hands.

43

The Paulista Who Was Born a Carioca

I often make bets with my clients about the schools that will accept them. It's a fun way to keep clients motivated and, most importantly, celebrate the outcome. I tend to win these bets, and I collect on them!

I remember well the case of Andrea from Banco Itaú, who wrote in her applications that her hobby was cooking. I bet her that if she got into Harvard, her biggest dream, she would have to prepare a dinner for me.

She became a student at Harvard, and, on one of my trips to Boston, I went to her house to collect on the bet. It was an extraordinary dinner, confirming the fact that she was a great cook.

There was also the case of Caielli, who wrote a memorable essay about the family custom of cooking as a team. He wrote that one of his greatest achievements was the day his family promoted him to lamb chef, which meant he would coordinate the laborious ritual previously conducted by his mother. The choice of seasoning, trimmings, and cooking time became his responsibility, all described with such enthusiasm that it led me to bet, of course, a leg of lamb if he got into Kellogg. I was unable to go to Evanston to collect on the bet, but as soon as he returns to Brazil, I will knock on his door.

Besides a wonderful chef, Caielli is an extremely resourceful and proactive person, qualities which I'm positive have contributed to his success. I recall that on the day of a group assessment conducted by our company for Banco Itaú—a very important part of the process to determine which candidates would receive sponsorship to get an MBA—he found himself stuck in a traffic jam (one of the downsides of living in São Paulo). Realizing that he would not make it in time, he had an extraordinary reaction. He parked his car, stopped a motorcyclist on the street, and offered him all his spare change to take him to where the assessment was to be held. He arrived disheveled and breathless, but strictly on schedule. The outcome? He got the sponsorship.

The third major food-loving client who came to me was Lauro, who was also sponsored by Banco Itaú. Interestingly, during the preparation phase, we would joke that he was a *Paulista* at heart. Being born in Rio was just an accident. He was so well suited to São Paulo that it was easy to forget his place of origin. He didn't even have a problem with the politically incorrect jokes about *Cariocas*. Instead of taking offense, he showed himself to be easygoing, kind, charming, and very intelligent. The great stories he wrote about his transition from Rio de Janeiro to São Paulo brought excellent results, with admission to several schools, including Harvard.

Our bet also involved a meal, but it was more original. We decided that if he was admitted to Harvard, we would celebrate the admission by having lunch at the dingy, corner bakery, as proof of humility. We talked about this jokingly, in the midst of other conversations, and time passed. Usually, after the applications are sent, we have to wait about three months for the answer, an eternity for those who are hoping for radical change in their lives.

The day he got a positive response from Harvard was a day that was much celebrated by all of us in my firm. Of the more than 120 employees from Banco Itaú whom we prepared for the MBA, only three got into Harvard. Lauro was one of them.

I had almost forgotten about the bet when Lauro called me asking if our lunch at the bakery was still on. We ate at the bar, standing. It was one of the best-tasting sandwiches I have eaten in my life. It tasted like victory.

44

A Brazilian Saga

Luis Cláudio belonged to a family who suffered much harassment from the media, since they were the main shareholders of a large bank. Some of his relatives, including his father, had died in a helicopter crash years before I met him. He had been educated by his uncle, who eventually entered into politics, becoming minister of agriculture. At the time of his MBA application process Luis Cláudio worked in the commercial area of the bank, preparing to assume a leadership position in the business. Despite being very young, he led a large team, acting as manager of one of the largest branches of the bank.

His academic training was excellent. He had graduated from the business school Fundação Getúlio Vargas (FGV-SP) and done internships in important companies, besides taking on significant entrepreneurial initiatives in the area of cable television and the Internet. He also had a good GMAT score. Our challenge was only to tell his story in as intriguing a manner as possible.

An analogy with the Kennedy family emerged from our brainstorming sessions. At the time, they had recently suffered one of the many tragedies that have marked this nearly royal American family. Despite the setbacks, a survivor always appeared carrying forward the mission of leadership the family exercised in the United States for decades.

In recounting the story of Luis Cláudio, including the fatal crash that killed the main leaders of the family business, we demonstrated the value of the people who were able to pick up the pieces and continue to play important roles in Brazilian society. We also explained that his career goals were linked to a succession plan within the financial arm of the group of companies controlled by the family.

Luis Cláudio was admitted to several universities. The admission to Columbia was particularly celebrated because his main goal was to live in New York City so that he could be close to the Wall Street environment, making him better prepared for a career in the bank.

Shortly after starting his MBA, a new setback brought even more dramatic colors to the saga that was his life—the sale of the bank.

Suddenly, Luis Cláudio found himself cut off from the opportunity to develop the career he had planned. Again, he demonstrated his ability to overcome obstacles, getting a great job in a French bank that was well established in the United States, BNP Paribas. This is one of the great advantages of doing an MBA at an internationally recognized school: it places the student in contact with numerous multinational employers, increasing global job opportunities and careers.

After living and working successfully for a few years in New York, Luis Cláudio returned to Brazil to assume an executive position at a major TV company in Parana. This career change was surely made possible by the experience he had acquired during his MBA.

45

The Creative Engineer

Luiz Fernando was a different kind of engineer. He had received his engineering degree from the Polytechnic Institute at the University of São Paulo and had been appointed by his employer to receive a full scholarship to do an MBA. The sponsorship award was based both on his excellent job performance and the results of the rigorous selection process conducted by our company, aiming to identify high-potential employee-candidates. That alone did not make him very different from other good engineers. Several of them had received sponsorship from Banco Itaú. This relatively large amount of sponsored candidates could even have the negative effect of making the honor less distinctive in the eyes of the admissions officers.

This was not the case with Luiz Fernando. His résumé had significant elements that set him apart from other candidates. For example, he showed entrepreneurial initiative even during his undergraduate studies when he created a shop with very particular characteristics. Being quite creative, he had identified an unexplored niche and used his engineering expertise to create and sell educational toys. He did not stop at that. Diversifying his areas of interest, he had written a book on emotional intelligence at a time when this subject was just beginning to attract attention in Brazil. Very eclectic, he had always been able to combine several activities simultaneously, developing his soft skills well.

He did his MBA at Carnegie Mellon, a school less well known in Brazil than, say, Harvard or MIT, yet with an excellent reputation in the USA and worldwide. It is especially strong in the areas of industrial management, production, and other specialties where quantitative tools are used. Returning to Brazil upon graduation, Luiz Fernando enjoyed rapid promotion, and soon reached a prominent executive position.

A curious fact concerning Luiz Fernando, was the work done by his wife while he was attending the MBA program. Luciana was a journalist who did freelance work for Brazilian publications. One of her projects involved comparing the different MBA programs available around the world. I read the original work and found it to be of very high quality. The article described the pros and cons of each school. To my surprise (and Luciana's too), the publisher who hired her services only published a part of what she had written, the part describing the MBA at Harvard. Those who read it got the false impression that Luciana was recommending the Harvard MBA as the best in the world, disregarding the excellence of other MBA programs.

We are often confronted with this kind of problem when we give interviews to newspapers and magazines, both in Brazil and abroad. Often the reporter has an agenda to follow and uses only the parts of the interview that support this agenda, thwarting the intention of the interviewee. Once, for example, after an interview of mine, a graph with the characteristics of each school was cited as being of my authorship. It was supposedly the key to success in the admissions process. I was very displeased when I read the article. It used snippets of things I had said in a different context, transforming them into the story.

Luiz Fernando and Luciana felt so hurt by the episode that they sent e-mails to everyone they knew, explaining the facts, and exposing the opportunism of the publisher who had distorted the report. For my part, I helped them by disclosing information at my disposal. That's when I started thinking about the possibility of enlisting Luciana's help with this book and including a comparison of the different MBAs. Later, as the work was taking shape, it became clear that my goal would not be to create one more MBA guide, of which there are so many on the market, but rather to convey my experience advising applicants. I decided to stick to the original idea.

What was very strong in me, however, was my great admiration for this couple who, like many others, experienced the MBA in all its fullness. They turned it into a life project; much more than a mere master's degree. This is what I try to communicate to the couples who come to me in increasing numbers. The MBA should be understood as an opportunity to grow together, a life-changing experience that enriches the couple intellectually and brings them closer.

46

Jack-of-All-Trades

There are many ways to stand out from the competition in any sphere of life. Professionally speaking, some choose the path of specialization, obtaining recognition for having profound knowledge about a certain subject. When I studied medicine, I contemplated following this path. I remember spending my spare time in a research laboratory for microsurgery, which was something very innovative at the time (nowadays, it is quite common). We worked with special lenses and nano-instruments to reconstruct arteries, veins, nerves, and lymphatic vessels, aiming at the reimplantation of amputated limbs. We would work for eight, even ten hours, in a one-centimeter surgical area, until we restored blood flow. I remember well the example of a firefighter whose wedding ring had gotten hooked on a ladder as he fell. I remember helping the micro-surgeon for hours in exchange for the reward of saving the man's ring finger.

Other people stand out for the multiplicity of their knowledge and skills. The general professional, whether in medicine or in any other industry, has been increasingly valued in organizations, given his or her flexibility and potential contribution in various areas, especially considering the constant fluctuation in demand for products and services that has become so characteristic of the modern business world.

Both the specialist and generalist models, of course, come with attendant risks. The specialist who is too exclusively centered on a specific area risks redundancy if the company changes its focus. The generalist, with his or her superficial knowledge of a lot of things, risks losing credibility. I believe that a professional manager needs to be a combination of these two models. The ideal manager should know a lot about a particular area but should not restrict him or herself to working only in that area. Outstanding managers accumulate knowledge of several other fields, aiming to lead people and processes regardless of their technical content. Generalists with various specialties are more valued than specialists in general matters. This difference is not subtle, and it favors the profile of what HR people call multispecialists.

✳   ✳   ✳

I met Marcelo during the Unibanco selection process, which had as its aim to define which employees would receive sponsorship to get their MBAs abroad. Our company is responsible for this type of process all over Brazil, and the evaluation techniques we use are quite diverse, including tests, interviews, group processes, and simulation games that seek to identify the competencies of each candidate, with special emphasis on leadership potential and capacity to handle the selection process of the best universities in the world.

At first a little shy, Marcelo loosened up during the process. He demonstrated great potential in his evaluation, combining strong analytical and quantitative skills with excellent performance in the group projects. He came out like a genius in the cognitive tests and led team exercises with ease, quickly earning credibility before his teammates. Upon reviewing his résumé, I was surprised to learn that he had studied public administration at the Fundação Getúlio Vargas and had done a specialization course in finance at the São Paulo-based business school INSPER (formerly IBMEC-SP). Given his ease with cognitive tasks, I had assumed that he had an engineering background.

It turned out he had started his career as a trainee at the Banco Nacional, having worked in several areas (mergers and acquisitions, treasury, corporate finance, international capital markets, and international treasury), always with excellent performance. One of his concerns when he was drafting his admission essays was to avoid casting his career progress in a negative light. He worried about the fact that he had made many switches, "leaping from branch to branch," as he put it. I made him see that, instead, he was becoming a multispecialist.

I was thrilled when he told me stories from his childhood, of times when he helped his father in an auto shop, learning to do things most of us would not dare try. Even before entering college, he was already a junior mechanic, a jack-of-all-trades who could do a bit of everything. This foreshadowed what would become his trademark versatility, a characteristic which we explored in his essays. His score of 770 on the GMAT, along with his wonderful stories and demonstrated multispecialist abilities, cemented his chances. He was admitted to all the schools he applied to: Stanford, Harvard, Wharton, Chicago, and Columbia.

The choice of Stanford eventually led Marcelo to other career changes, often radical but always successful. He withdrew from Unibanco to help create a telecommunications and IT startup for the Promon Group, a major Brazilian player in the field of technology. He was responsible for the financial area of the new company. After a year, he took over as the CFO of the group, and in 2004, became executive director responsible for finances, HR, systems, and administration, managing a team of eighty people and reporting to the president. Then he was hired as CFO of Lambert-Dodart-Chancereul (LDC), a large multinational group of French origin, operating in the agribusiness industry. Marcelo is responsible for finance, controllership, taxes, IT, risk management, HR, and strategic planning in Brazil; and is a member of the LDC Global Executive Committee, proving once again the value of a multispecialist in the business world.

47

The Family Business Dilemma

Marcello Z. was one of several of my clients whose families own thriving businesses. Not all such potential successors have great clarity about the goals of their career, and Marcello Z. was among those divided on this issue, a circumstance more common than most people would imagine. Many of the heirs of family enterprises whom I have met have faced the dilemma of choosing to follow in the footsteps of those who preceded them or having independent careers.

When I went to a talk in São Paulo given by Professor John Davis—a Harvard professor considered the highest authority in the world on the subject of family businesses—I was very impressed by his take on the issue of succession. He presented statistics showing that most family businesses succumb in the third generation; few survive until the fourth generation.

He explained that the main problem was that the businesses had difficulties from the challenge to grow at the same rate and speed as the demand for resources from the growing family. Subsequent generations tend to consume more than the company can provide. In many cases, the firm, by accepting poorly qualified family members as employees, ends up generating conflicts that often lead to bankruptcy or hasten the dissolution of the business.

However, there are notable exceptions. The speaker gave the example of the Dutch family that has been successfully managing the previously mentioned clothing retailer C&A for 160 years. He also mentioned certain entrepreneurs of Korean origin whose company has been a world leader in the production of soy sauce for over four

139

hundred years. There are several other examples, some of them in Brazil. Professor Davis says these companies remain productive by deploying very well-managed succession processes with clear rules about the participation of relatives in the business. In these cases, there are so many restrictions that it is often harder for a family member to join the company than someone selected from the labor market. Requirements, such as the excellence of the universities attended, MBA programs abroad, years of work experience, fluency in foreign languages, and so on, limit the access of poorly prepared family members, ensuring the quality of the company's future leaders.

The company run by Marcello's family is one of the Brazilian cases of continuous success. The company has only grown since its founding in 1905. Marcello's great-grandfather, a pharmacist of great vision, had decreed that his small business in the city of Araraquara should concern itself above all with the customers, prioritizing their needs before any sale. He could hardly have imagined that his descendants, a century later, would be managing a chain of 135 stores and almost three thousand employees, guided by those same principles, passed down from generation to generation.

I learned all about it from Marcello, the youngest brother of the fourth generation on the maternal side. He had grown up listening to these and other compelling stories. His father, who had died early, had also had a strong influence on him. Besides being a distinguished professor, he had been an entrepreneur and significant political leader, Minister of State for Science and Technology, Director of the University of São Paulo (USP) Polytechnic Institute, and founder of a successful construction company.

Marcello Z. and his brothers had exemplary educations. Attending the best schools, participating in exchange programs, and studying languages, they were prepared to face any kind of career inside or outside the family business.

When his father passed away, Marcello Z. had just started his university studies in business at FGV-SP. He then became greatly influenced by his two older brothers. Both worthy examples, they had had great work experience outside the family business. After doing MBAs in well-ranked schools—MIT and the University of Michigan—they had joined the drugstore chain, where they built successful careers alongside cousins who had received education of a similar level.

The main difficulty in the application was related to Marcello's transcript from FGV. Shaken by the recent death of his father, and unsure of his career choice, he had dedicated himself more to internships than classes, getting only average grades as a result. He had interned in great companies in the retail and consulting industries before joining the commercial department of the drugstore, qualifying himself for career prospects either inside or outside the family business.

We decided to focus on the issue of family succession in his essays, acknowledging the uncertainties about the future, but admitting the possibility of a career in the family business. Following in the footsteps of one of his brothers, he ended up getting his MBA at the University of Michigan, a great school that excels in many areas of expertise. There, to cite one example, taught Professor C. K. Prahalad, the leading authority on strategic planning and author of the highly successful *Wealth at the Bottom of the Pyramid.*

I was very happy when I learned that Marcello Z. graduated with distinction from the MBA program. This, in my view, shows that, once he overcame the trauma of his father's death, and brought his greater maturity to bear, he was able to concentrate on his studies and realize his full academic potential.

Nowadays, he works for Borders, the second-largest book retailer at the time, now owned by Barnes & Noble. If he decides in the future to go back to the business that his great-grandfather started, he will have accumulated solid international experience and certainly will help the team of superstars in his family prove that it is possible to perpetuate a successful family business beyond the third generation.

48

The *Pernambucano*

The first time I heard about the specialization of Executive Development was when my wife coordinated a study at Banco Itaú that aimed to identify young talents and develop their management skills to assume leadership positions within the organization in the future. At that time, I was a newly graduated physician and was serving a one-year term in the army as lieutenant-doctor. Inevitably, I suppose, I contrasted the military system with the civilian meritocratic system. In most countries, a military career is based on length of service, giving military personnel the security of knowing that, so long as they do not break any rules, they will be promoted through the ranks. In such circumstances, there is little or no institutional incentive for them to seek professional development.

A good system of executive development, by contrast, encourages people with high potential to pursue their own growth, a very healthy practice for both employees and organizations. Years later, far from the military environment, I experienced in my own consulting firm the rewarding feeling that comes from witnessing the rapid growth of people who are even sometimes unaware of their own abilities and potential. The *Pernambucano* was one of these cases.

Our consultants were providing an assessment service for Banco Itaú in northeastern Brazil. During work carried out in the city of Recife in the state of Pernambuco, Paulo P., a local engineer, stood out from the others, drawing the attention of our staff. Recently graduated, he worked in plant maintenance for the bank branches, being called whenever infrastructure problems arose—from power outages to leaky pipes. These were tasks that rarely challenged someone so highly qualified. He was, therefore, somewhat discouraged, knowing that his full capabilities were being underutilized.

As soon as our assessment system identified him as a high-potential employee, we designed an action plan to accelerate his career development. One of the obstacles encountered was that he was somewhat acculturated to the situation, seeing his work as a job, not as a career. When we suggested that he move to São Paulo, he initially resisted the idea, not enthusiastic about leaving his home, friends, and fiancée. However, after discussing the future possibilities that could potentially include funding for a master's degree abroad, he decided to give his best to a project that would be the most radical change in career to date.

In São Paulo, as agreed, after a year of work marked by outstanding performance, Paulo P. was selected to receive sponsorship from the bank to commence an MBA program.

One obstacle he faced was his lack of fluency in English. However, by studying hard—something he was very good at—he managed to overcome this deficiency and do well on the GMAT. At the end of the process, his offer of admission to MIT was much celebrated. He accepted this offer from among those of several other schools that had also admitted him based on his history of overcoming obstacles and seeking professional growth. I was amused when he phoned to tell me about Duke, the first school that offered him admission. He called me up and said, in that relaxed manner from northeastern Brazil, "I got into Dúque!" just like that, with his northeastern accent alive and well.

After MIT, he continued his career at Banco Itaú, accumulating expertise in different fields and later being hired by the C&A bank. He has since moved to another bank in southern Brazil. I'm sure that if Paulo P. had refused to broaden his horizons and move to a larger city, he would not have developed so rapidly, perhaps never reaching the positions he reached. Nowadays, he is a finance professional with the status, training, and credentials to work anywhere in the world.

49

The King of Agribusiness

Whenever I encounter someone involved in agribusiness, I feel elated, for the chances of having different, interesting stories in that segment are always significant, and being different and interesting are always virtues in the MBA admissions game. Clients in agribusiness have never disappointed me in this regard.

Pedro was one of those cases; in fact, he is the one agribusiness client who surpassed them all. Hence the title *King* which I attributed to him in this chapter. His story is as follows:

His father, one of many Japanese immigrants who found wealth in Brazilian agribusiness, created a group of companies based in the state of Goias that ended up taking the lead in various related sectors in Brazil. An international ranking once placed this group as one of the major cotton producers in the world; it also had extensive participation in soybean plantations and the production of hydrogenated products, among other activities.

But this success story was also marked by tragedy. A plane crash had killed several family members, including Pedro's eldest brother, who had been chosen as his father's successor in the family business. Suddenly, Pedro and his other brothers were given the responsibility of planning the succession of the group, filling the gap left by the brother who had been ready to take on the challenge.

Pedro was the family member with the best academic foundation. In his youth, he had moved to São Paulo to study business at FGV, preparing himself to be an effective administrator. He had learned English and read everything he could about the gurus of management, dreaming of studying abroad one day. But his responsibilities to his family prevented him from realizing his dream, until the change in succession opened up new possibilities.

When he came to me, he knew very clearly that he wished to get his graduate degree at a top-caliber school. He had the approval of his family, who agreed he should be as well qualified as possible to run the business. The great obstacle, however, was his age. Already in his forties, even though he had a youthful appearance, Pedro did not fit the typical candidate profile for top MBA courses, where the average age is around twenty-eight. In my view, he had no hope of admission to the schools that comprised his wish list. Moreover, he did not feel that he could devote a full two years to meeting his educational objectives.

The solution was to guide him to do a course called the Sloan Fellows Program, which is offered in only three universities in the world: MIT, Stanford, and London Business School. The one-year course is designed for people with at least ten years' professional experience and proven performance in leadership positions.

The reason it is possible to attain this degree in just one year is that some of the more basic subjects are not included, based on the premise that an experienced manager has already mastered these topics. There is also no focus on finding a job afterward, since almost all students are sponsored by their employers and plan to return to their companies upon completion of the program.

A compelling aspect of the Sloan Fellows Program is the level of networking it fosters. All participants are in much more advanced stages of professional development than students in a traditional course. This means that they have many connections to offer, increasing the potential benefits of their network.

Pedro liked the idea and embraced the challenge of applying. He was then admitted to both programs that he applied to: Stanford and MIT. He chose the former and had a wonderful experience, not just academic and professional, but also personal, since he took his wife and teenage children with him, and they all enjoyed the excellent quality of life in Palo Alto, California.

By the time he got back to Brazil, Pedro had already established himself as a leader in agribusiness, serving on the boards of numerous companies, besides continuing to work in the family business.

We're still in frequent contact, and I can say I learned a lot about agribusiness and the leadership of family businesses from him. I feel rewarded for helping him find the optimal path for his development at a critical moment in his career.

50

The Can That Made the Man

In the role of educational consultant, I have learned that ascending careers are not necessarily seen by admissions officers as ideal. Career growth alone is not sufficient if applicants lack solid examples of leadership, teamwork, and people management.

I encountered this circumstance when I met Marcos. Clearly a high-potential candidate, he was endowed with quick and unclouded thinking abilities and was bound for the fast track. Besides being extremely friendly, outgoing, and talkative, he had a wonderful sense of humor and a captivating wit.

From his simulated tests emerged another good surprise. One of the parts of the GMAT that most terrifies people is reading comprehension, which requires the ability to draw quick conclusions based on a short article. He did wonderfully well on that section. He even tried to harness this ability of his to help others by teaching speed-reading skills.

However, there were some obstacles. The first was a manifest lack of dedication to his studies. He had worked full time from early on to help with the finances at home. As a result, he obtained lower grades than expected and took longer than usual to graduate.

The second obstacle was his professional career. He started his corporate life early by working as an auditor for PriceWaterhouseCoopers. Next, he had worked as assistant controller of PepsiCo for a year, and then moved on to Latapack, a multinational manufacturer of aluminum cans for Pepsi and other companies, where he had been for about three years. His strong performance had led him to several achievements: he had become a full-time employee before graduating from college and had received rapid promotion, reaching the position of senior analyst, where the only person working above him was the area director. Because he worked for an American company, he wrote his reports and analyses in English and then forwarded them to the US headquarters.

However, no matter how we told his story, we ended up describing a bureaucratic career with little managerial responsibilities or leadership practice. We needed something more, something that would show Marcos's creativity, a quality that I knew existed in him, but that was underrepresented on paper. His high GMAT score, achieved on the first try, counterbalanced his college grades, but were insufficient to have the same impact on his work history. Besides, Marcos was very ambitious and wanted to change the direction of his career—he wanted to work in the financial markets, preferably in a large multinational bank.

The NYU application, with its "describe yourself creatively to colleagues" question, once again gave me the opportunity to help make a candidate shine. With it, Marcos caught the attention of the admissions officers once and for all.

In our brainstorming session, we got the idea of using an aluminum can to describe him. The label on the can showed his picture, the NYU logo, and the ingredients: *motivation 100%, leadership 100%*, and so forth. Incidentally, this was the original idea which later inspired similar cases, like the medicine carton described in a previous chapter.

The project required significant effort. He had to convince his colleagues at the company to create a photolithography just for him. It is not easy to stop the production line of an industry that produces thousands of units per day with the aim of producing a single can, different from all the others. This was only possible thanks to Marcos's engaging personality, which had helped him make good friends at work.

The final product was a professionally produced can with the Pepsi colors and a slot on the lid to insert coins. Marcos's reasoning: the admissions officers at NYU would not be able to file the can, so they would probably leave it on top of a desk for the duration of the admission process. In that case, it was best if the can had a function—that of a piggy bank—so they would not forget him so easily. Besides, his goal was banking; so such a can presented a complete image.

In fact, they did not forget. He was admitted to NYU where, after an excellent MBA focused on finance, he was hired by Citibank in New

York. He continued his ascending career, becoming vice president of the treasury of the Citi Consumer Bank, one of the most coveted domains in the United States. He returned to Brazil with a résumé that was the envy of any professional in the finance market.

I always discuss that can with new clients who feel insecure about their professional history. And herein lies the debate: to what extent did the can make the man? I do not know, nor will I ever know. It may not have had any impact whatsoever, since Marcos had the qualities needed to be successful, as demonstrated by his career after the MBA.

In this line of work, however, we are dealing with the unpredictable, with the subjective, with perceptions. It is possible that on the day when Marcos's material was analyzed, among thousands of other files from around the world, the can stood out, bringing the right kind of attention to his strengths. I prefer to believe this hypothesis. Besides being very entertaining, the idea has afforded us, over the years, with other positive results in the competitive admissions game.

51

Chasing Pearls

Every time I come across extraordinary people who come to me asking for advice, I think about how difficult it must be for admission officers to choose a limited number of applicants every year. Having so much power over the fate of people is a tremendous responsibility, especially when the selection criteria are highly subjective. The job of finding the pearls to send to these officers, however, is very rewarding. It requires, above all, patience—not always is what we seek evident at first sight. Sometimes however, the details of a candidate's story are so striking that they become imprinted on our brains forever.

The association of ideas is a powerful mechanism for memorization. Who doesn't remember what they were doing during the attack on 9/11 or, for Brazilians, on the day of Ayrton Senna's death? I, for example, remember the trivial things I was doing on those days, which under normal circumstances I would have long ago forgotten. In a lesser way, though crucial to a single candidate, it is precisely this effect that we seek to make on the admissions officer.

Based on numbers I've studied concerning the workload of admissions officers, I estimate that an MBA admissions officer reads on average, fifteen to twenty applications per day, resulting in a scarce forty to fifty minutes devoted to each candidate. In less than an hour, the officers must consider four or five essays, two or three letters of recommendation, a résumé, transcripts, TOEFL and GMAT scores, and a plethora of other documents, and then be able to pronounce a verdict at the end of the analysis. It is reasonable to assume that candidates without striking stories will be forgotten and discarded, without mercy or the right to appeal.

The reverse is a more-than-reasonable assumption: applicants with striking stories are still remembered by the end of the day and become the only ones with a chance of admission. Our initial task, therefore, is to hook the attention of the admissions officer, either through novelty, excitement, surprise, or admiration.

I remember to this day, for example, the woman who was a descendant of a samurai, and who, still living with her family, contemplated every day the sword her father had inherited and that hung on the wall of the family living room. That sword stirred in her emotions that marked her life. On the one hand, it symbolized the values of the samurai transmitted across generations—values of loyalty, bravery, and persistence. On the other hand, it provoked uncomfortable feelings over the sexism that prevented her from inheriting the object simply for being a woman.

The sword ended up being a source of motivation. It stimulated her from childhood to study more than the boys and to win all the prizes at school. It was the desire to prove her worth that led her to win, for example, the Mathematics Olympics in her hometown and later in the whole state. The same sentiment led to her success in the FGV admissions exam.

I'm sure that this story helped the woman get into MIT, just as their stories helped the Russian prince, the French nobleman, the general's son, the volunteer in Nepal, the girl from Pantanal, the jungle boy, the Bill Gates from Ceará, the daughter of the governor, the Shinto monk, the sons of the former Brazilian president, the Tylenol girl, the Jersey cattle rancher, the female rodeo champion, the reporter in the Middle East, the casino builder in Las Vegas, the girl from the town of Americana, the horse-riding champion, the nightclub owner, the trash specialist, the founder of the Japanese restaurant, and so many others who were admitted to the best schools in the world. There are enough characters to fill several books. Names and faces that are burned into my memory. Every year, I feel fortunate to be able to help people realize the value of their achievements and lead them to demonstrate their potential for business and management so that they can be admitted at an MBA program where they can acquire the skills and contacts to positively impact the greater community around them. I am grateful that, almost without realizing it, I discovered my own path, far from the original path which, thankfully, I had the courage to leave behind.

52

The Voice of the Client

When planning this book, we had the happy idea of distributing a questionnaire to the people we were considering including to ask their opinions about what the MBA experience represented in their lives and also for any advice they might offer to those who were thinking of treading the same path.

The answers were so interesting and well prepared that they could fill a guide or manual on the subject of pursuing an MBA in the USA, a project that I might consider undertaking in the future. Though equally valuable, it would be different from what we set out to do in this book, which was to record and transmit memories accumulated over more than twenty years of advising clients. Furthermore, many reports were similar, especially those that confirmed the relevance of the MBA in their lives. This gave us a practical problem: how should we use such rich material without seeming repetitive or being redundant?

After much deliberation, we decided to select the phrases that we considered most representative and outstanding, avoiding duplications, and classifying them into groups according to criteria of affinity and content. The title for each group reflects its respective theme, as follows:

The MBA: much more than an academic experience

- Think of the MBA as a life plan and engage long-term vision about it. Although the MBA student is generally very rational and always wants to calculate the ROI, feasibility, etc., it is important to understand that the experience can add a lot of intangible value to a person's life; value which is not immediately apparent upon graduation. (Denis Morante)

- Try to understand that the MBA is a comprehensive experience. If the justification or reason to do it is only professional, only personal, or only academic, it is just not worth it. But if it is a union of several factors, there is no experience quite like it! (David Turkie)
- You have to have something more in mind than just earning more money and getting a better job. The MBA has to be part of a broader goal in life, that of improving, growing, becoming almost another person. (Marcos Olmos)
- Think of the MBA as a means to improve yourself in order to achieve a larger goal in your professional life. Do not treat the MBA as a goal in itself. It should be a means, not an end. (Osvaldo Ribeiro)
- Do not think that the MBA is a passport to go live in the USA. Few foreigners find work or a visa to stay—even those who went to Harvard! (Bernard La Tour d'Auvergne)

Factors to consider to make the right decision

- Do not consider only the rankings when deciding about a program. A program can be perfect for some and bad for others. Choose programs according to their profiles. Early in the process of applying, schools may seem very similar, but in reality, there are big differences between them. (Marcello Zagottis)
- The Brazilian idea of an MBA is very different from the reality. I advise anyone who wants to make the best decision to come and visit the schools and talk to students, attend classes, participate in activities. Often the school that seems ideal on paper is not a good fit with your personal style or with your career goals. I am a living example of this: I was disappointed with some schools that were my favorites and I was positively surprised with others. (Alexandre Campos)

Decisive factors for admission

- Professionally, I've done very different things: I played tennis, representing Brazil in championships; worked as a set designer, illustrator, and art teacher; founded and managed a nonprofit for three years; and had a rich experience as a consultant in projects in Brazil and other countries. Academically, I had a good story: first place in the admission exam for USP, top-ranked at FGV, 750 on the GMAT. Besides, I planned my preparation in advance, which gave me time to write the essays calmly and properly prepare for exams. (Cláudio Sassaki)
- Being a person with diverse activities outside of work; e.g., professional keyboardist for six years, commercial pilot (to present), owner of a horseback-riding center, and practitioner of equestrian riding for almost ten years; languages—French, Spanish, English, etc. (Carlos Filgueiras)
- I believe it was my track record as industry leader in Brazilian agribusiness, and also because I could represent the agribusiness sector, which traditionally provides few MBA students. (Pedro Maeda)
- The fact that I was trained by the army and became a second lieutenant of the reserve army was a factor that set me apart from other applicants. Unlike Brazil, being part of the army is considered an important activity by Americans, valued because of the discipline that is required, the ability to work under pressure, military experience and so on . . . Another point that helped me a lot was the fact that I played water polo for ten years. For me it was a big surprise, because in Brazil, the army and sports are not highly valued. (Marcos Bellizia)
- I think it was certainly my story, along with the good work done in telling it in the applications, as well as my test scores. In Brazil, it is hard to find young successful entrepreneurs (by that I mean a story with a beginning, middle, and end), which is more common in the United States. I think they (admissions) appreciate that a lot. (Cristiano Câmera)
- I had a different story to tell, despite having worked in a common company in a common area. My trajectory was different because it was faster than usual and revealed that I am

a person who constantly seeks new challenges. This assured the admissions officers that I would be likely to seek activities off the beaten path during and after my MBA. (Denis Morante)
- Having been an active volunteer worker. (Fernanda Kattar Petto)

Advice to increase chances of admission

- None of the aspects of the application can guarantee a spot in a first-rate MBA program, be it the GMAT, TOEFL, the essays, the academic background, the letters of recommendation, or the interviews. However, any one of these aspects individually is capable of eliminating someone from the selection process. Therefore, a good mix of at least average performance in several aspects is essential. Finding an experienced consultant who can guide the applicant in all stages of the process is critical. (Artur Regen)
- I recommend that the candidate invests in a trip to visit the schools to which he or she is applying. Going there and showing your face conveys the impression to the recruiter that you are seriously interested in the school and would definitely accept an invitation to enroll there (the worst thing for a recruiter is to have an admission offer refused by the applicant). (Artur Regen)
- Do not be discouraged if you do not get a good score on the GMAT. When I did the test the first time I got a 620, even though I was getting a 720 on the practice tests. I thought that was impossible; so I did it again and got a 630. It was a huge disappointment. I studied for another month and, on the third attempt, I managed to raise my score on the GMAT to 700. (Carlos Filgueiras)
- Research the school and the program well before applying. It is essential to talk to former students and people who can tell you details of the day-to-day during the program. Understand the language used in the program and school. Take note of the subjects that might interest you. After having collected all this knowledge, the essays become more convincing. (Bernard La Tour d'Auvergne)

Prospects after the MBA

- I believed in the return on investment, sold everything I owned and did my MBA in the United States. The ROI began to bear fruit with my first summer internship. I got three job offers, all of them from large multinational companies. Moreover, in just one year my salary increased 200 percent, demonstrating the strength and recognition of an MBA in the labor market. (Osmar de Carvalho Santos Junior)

Encouraging comments

- If you are admitted, be prepared for the best two years of your life. It will be worth every day that you studied for the GMAT and did not sleep to write the applications. Too bad it's only two years! (Fernanda Kattar Petto)
- The MBA was, without doubt, the best experience of my life, and I advise all professionals who want to develop their careers to do an MBA at a good school. (Rodrigo Martins)
- The motives are so many. To experience life abroad, hear what the best have to say, be in contact with Nobel Prize winners, and to understand complex finances were perhaps the most important. (Rodolfo Fischer)
- In my experience, the two years in which you stay out of the labor market will be the richest years of your life in terms of knowledge acquired and methods of work/study learned. The things you learn are things that you usually do not learn alone. And you can't argue with the experience acquired by living outside your home country. Besides, you have a lifetime to keep working. (Marcos Bellizia)

Other comments

- Have a rich and unique history to tell . . . and tell it with passion. Make the school feel that not having you there will be a great loss. If you do not have a rich and unique story to tell, start creating one by living it. (Romilson Bastos)

53

Global Recognition and the Birth of AIGAC

For some time, the fact that I had invented a new profession that didn't even have a name bothered me. My work was linked to education and career development, and I served as a coach to my clients. I had several colleagues, some of whom had been my pupils, but I did not know anyone else who performed this same role in other countries.

In early 2005, round about March or April, I received an invitation from Tuck—the oldest MBA program and part of Dartmouth University, an Ivy League school—to attend a conference for educational advisors. It was the first time that a reputed school had recognized the importance of the profession and decided to organize an event for it, bringing together my peers from around the world.

The school paid for everything: airfare, ground transportation, the hotel stay, and meals. They brought the best professionals in this field to Hanover, New Hampshire. The group of twenty-five advisors enjoyed two intense days of seminars and workshops where we had contact with teachers, students, and school staff who shared with us the details of the Tuck MBA experience. I had long admired this school based on praise from alumni and the general market, but I began to admire it even more after this initiative, which represented a strong endorsement of our professional role.

It required of Tuck both vision and courage to organize this event. Some famous schools were choosing to ignore the existence of advisors like me, considering themselves self-sufficient in attracting and motivating candidates with the desired profile. We, on the other hand, believe that schools do not have the local knowledge and outreach necessary to do this job effectively all around the world.

During the Tuck event, I realized that talented people are working in several countries with common goals and similar techniques. The South Korean advisor, for example, was also a former MIT student, and many others had studied at Wharton, UCLA, Harvard, and other well-ranked schools. Many were former admissions officers from major schools and, thus, knew in depth the details of the selection process, contributing to the success of the candidates they helped.

One of these professionals, the American, Linda Abraham, had founded, roughly ten years prior, the website *accepted.com*, through which she provided the same type of admissions-consulting services for MBAs and other postgraduate courses that I offered. Nowadays, it is one of the largest services of its kind in the world, receiving hundreds of thousands of visits per year and serving clients in numerous countries. I met Linda at the Tuck event and we immediately became friends, bonded by the similarity in our work, values, philosophy, and ethics.

Together, we had the idea to create a nonprofit organization to establish universal criteria for our profession and its ethical standards, as well as promoting discussion among the professionals who we decided to call "admissions consultants."

The following year, two more outstanding professionals joined us. The extremely competent Maxx Duffy, a former Harvard admissions officer who now serves as a boutique consultant to clients in the United States and many other countries, including Brazil. The other very well-qualified professional who joined us was Graham Richmond. He graduated from Wharton, where he worked in the admissions department, and later created a software that quickly became very popular in the world of MBAs—the Multi-App—which served to facilitate the process of filling out several applications at the same time. Graham and another partner also created the website ClearAdmit.com. Similar to Linda Abraham's website, it is now one of the largest in the world, with a very large customer base in Europe. Despite living in Paris, he spends a good part of his time in Philadelphia, creating a commute as unlikely as Lucca-São Paulo.

This was the team of professionals invited in June of 2006 to do a presentation together in San Francisco, California, at the biggest global event for admission consultants—the GMAC Congress. GMAC is the entity that is responsible for the GMAT, TOEFL, SAT, and many other standardized tests that are used to compare applicants across the world. Seven hundred professionals from around the world attended the event. Among admissions consultants, I was the only Latin American representative.

The event was so important to us that we decided to get together the night before at Linda's home in Los Angeles to rehearse our presentation, which had already been carefully prepared over two months through several conference calls. I remember the day was particularly picturesque. Since it was my wife's birthday, Linda invited us both to dinner at the Milky Way, a restaurant in California that is owned by Stephen Spielberg's mother. The menu was kosher and Ms. Spielberg herself greeted us at the entrance and helped us choose our dishes. She is extremely joyful and talkative, petite and energetic, the kind of person who doesn't miss an opportunity to make a joke. Among the jokes she told that night was that Stephen had been very strange as a child, but fortunately he refused to see a psychologist. Thanks to his eccentricity, he created ET and entertained millions of people, becoming a millionaire in the process!

The next day, our presentation was very successful. We had the privilege of having lunch with the directors of admissions of the top-ten schools, many of whom started to support our work from then on. From these meetings and conversations arose the organization mentioned above, which we named AIGAC (Association of International Graduate Admissions Consultants) and registered in Sacramento, California, where our headquarters are located. AIGAC was founded in November 2006 and our website was officially launched in early May, 2007 (www. aigac.org). Linda was our first president, followed by Graham, and then Anna Ivey. I've been a member of the board of directors since then, besides being one of two non-American representatives among the directors.

I reproduce below part of the article published in the official GMAC newspaper (*GMAC News*), which summarized my participation in the San Francisco event:

> Ricardo Betti of MBA Empresarial, Brazil, discussed the
> various ways in which admissions consultants can help

applicants navigate the application process. The consultants assist in-self assessment, assisting candidates in exploring different career alternatives. They also monitor the construction of oral and written skills, and support the revision of essays to better reflect the writers' experience and represent themselves accurately. Betti's company also promotes relationships with institutions and companies for the purpose of placing candidates in jobs after the MBA. Betti offers career advice and networking for the rest of a client's life. Consultants and clients celebrate together the success of each candidate in the MBA and in seeking employment after the course. He sees his company as an ally to admissions officers since both are interested in helping candidates make the most of business school and their résumé.

In addition to the international prominence that this congress has brought us, it helped us, especially, to organize and systematize the profession in the global scene, establishing best practices and standards of ethical conduct that had never been discussed nor consolidated in a forum of such magnitude and scope. Taking part in the launch and consolidation of AIGAC is one of the things I most cherish in my career as a graduate admissions consultant.

We currently have eighty-seven members across the globe, having organized conferences for four consecutive years, which were hosted by some of the best reputed business schools: Chicago Booth jointly with Kellogg, Columbia with NYU Stern, MIT Sloan with HBS, and Stanford GSB with Berkeley-Haas. Our conferences have been attended by admission consultants from all over the world, as well as by directors of admissions from renowned universities.

Today, I am confident that everything was worth it in this path that I chose, helping hundreds of Brazilians to internationalize their careers and become world citizens.

54

Setting an Example

One of the best consequences of the path that I took was the example I set for my children. Convinced, as my wife and I are, of the importance of learning languages and studying abroad, they have exceeded our expectations, becoming true citizens of the world from early on, prepared to face life anywhere on the map.

Our son, Mauricio, who was born in 1982, has always been a great student. He studied at FGV-SP and received several scholarships in high school and college, including one to spend a semester at Bocconi University in Milan. Soon after graduation, with another scholarship from FGV, he attended a one-year master's program in Europe, in the area of international business, spending six months studying in Rotterdam (Erasmus) and six months in Barcelona (ESADE). He worked for two years at Bain & Company, an American strategic consulting firm, and almost three years at the Spanish telecom giant Telefonica, in which his outstanding performance resulted in a Top Quality Improvement Project award that included sponsored vacations abroad. At less than thirty years of age, he is totally fluent in four languages, being completely self-sufficient and capable to work in Brazil and abroad with the same efficiency. He is currently pursuing his MBA at MIT Sloan.

Our daughter, Renata, who was born in 1984, was also always a good student, and participated in several exchange programs starting as a teenager. Besides spending a semester of high school in the United States and two summers with her brother in Canada and Australia, she holds two undergraduate degrees (social communication and journalism). She worked at the international nonprofit Endeavor for a year, during which time our whole family became volunteers at the institution. Next, she went to live in England, where she spent a year as a visiting student at Westminster University in London. There she kept busy with eight different classes over the course of a year and in her role as student ambassador, for which she was chosen by the university.

After graduation, Renata was hired by the largest publishing house in Brazil, Editora Abril, becoming a reporter for the widely read, general news magazine *Veja*. There she engaged in a brilliant career, moving to Rio de Janeiro and being awarded two prizes—Best Article in Education and the Study Abroad Award, which materialized in a journalism summer course at Harvard University, sponsored by Editora Abril.

There is a great story about my kids that happened when they were studying in Europe in 2005. The Gillette company held a contest for their employees around the world in which the winners would spend three days in Madrid, getting VIP treatment, staying in a five-star hotel, doing limousine tours around town, watching the Real Madrid soccer team practice, and spending an afternoon with David Beckham, learning from him how to kick penalty shots on the Real Madrid field.

Winners in several countries were invited to the event, including Portuguese, Brazilians, Spaniards, and Scandinavians, many of whom did not speak English. Since David Beckham speaks only English, the event organizers decided to recruit translator-interpreters among college students who were in Europe at that time. Once my kids heard about this opportunity, they sent their résumés and were hired to earn about three hundred euros to be available during three days, with reimbursement for accommodation and meals.

Result: the two had an incredible experience, saw all of Madrid from the window of a limousine, interacted with David Beckham, taking pictures with him, and learning the best technique for a penalty kick on a grassy field. Actually, my daughter did not learn. She was wearing platform shoes, one of which fell off when she went in for the kick, causing her to fall flat on her face on the grass. Beckham very politely helped her get up, but not before having a good laugh. Unfortunately, she didn't get a chance to redeem herself since there were a lot of people in line behind her . . .

Upon seeing the pictures of my kids with Beckham, many friends commented on their luck. I believe, however, that this kind of opportunity comes to those who are not only in the right place at the right time, but are fully prepared to face any challenges. Fluency in foreign languages and the resourcefulness acquired through international experiences were key factors in this endeavor, and had little to do with luck. They are the fruit of our beliefs and efforts in acquiring the status of citizens of the world, values that I've been passing to clients for nearly twenty-four years and which, fortunately, we were also able to transmit to our children. We are very proud of them!

55

Under the Tuscan Sun

It would be impossible to complete my first book without talking about my Italian origins. I grew up hearing stories about Lucca, the Tuscan town where my father's ancestors were born. My first trip abroad, the result of a contest at school about Italian colonization in Brazil, could not have had a better beginning—the house of my relatives in Lucca. I was only sixteen, and I was impressed by everything I saw. After exploring Lucca and its surroundings for two weeks, I went to see the rest of Europe, a two-month backpacking trip. It was an experience that would mark my life forever.

Traveling alone is not easy. Coming face to face with the gorgeous walls of Lucca or with a magnificent field of sunflowers and not having a friend along to share that moment can be frustrating at best. On the other hand, there is nothing like the enjoyment of the sense of freedom and independence that soon develops on a trip like this; it is a feeling that also leaves its mark on the mind and soul of the traveler, bringing self-confidence and the certainty of being able to solve any problem. That first trip had this effect on my personality, which would eventually be reflected in many decisions I made in my life in order to build my future. Sometimes I have contradicted the opinion of the majority, but I've always stayed true to my values, aspirations, and vocations.

At forty, with my life already consolidated and with teenage children, my wife, Sandra, planned a trip that ended up being the best of my life: We took my parents to Italy, where we rented a car and traversed the country, showing them the cities that they had always dreamed of seeing and, of course, visiting our relatives in Lucca. My mother had corresponded all her life with these cousins of my father, and finally had the chance to know them personally—it was one of the greatest moments of her life. My kids also loved this trip and still enjoy the memories, especially the funny comments made by my father, the *nonno*, which today have become part of the list of favorite family anecdotes and will certainly be passed on to future generations.

All these interactions with Tuscany, especially Lucca, had the effect of awakening my desire to know more and better the land where my family had come from. It was the ideal setting to finish my book, where I would tell the experiences of many people who I helped over the years and explore a few of my experiences with them.

The premature death of my brother, Roberto, at fifty-four years of age, left several of his life projects unfinished. Fluent in several languages, also a world citizen, and about to graduate in literature and pursue his dream of teaching Latin at the University of São Paulo, he suffered a fatal stroke in 2007. Besides the pain of his loss, his death triggered in me a deep process of reflection that compelled me to pursue two of the projects that I considered of major importance in my life, but that the everyday business of running a company did not allow me to give their due priority—completing this book and doing further research on my family roots.

Thus, with my family supporting the idea, in April of 2007 I left for another adventure, alone again, just as on my journey at sixteen years old. I moved to Lucca and, with Sandra's help, found the ideal place for my sabbatical and to finish my projects.

For a year, I lived in a studio on the ground floor of a building in the final phase of restoration (Palazzo Bottini), located in the historic center of Lucca. It is near the Amphitheatre Piazza, which I used as my office, seeking inspiration to write. The medieval atmosphere of the city, the beautiful walls, the music of Puccini, the exceptional restaurants, the tastes and smells of Tuscany, everything, in fact, contributed to making this experience unique. Every day I fell more in love with that place, and I felt invigorated to write, away from the stress of São Paulo and Brazil's ills.

I often had dinner with cousins in the house where I had stayed thirty-five years before. It's a big house with three floors, each designed to house an entire family. The person who built this house was the family patriarch, my great-grandfather, Egisto Betti, who emigrated to

Brazil and later, already rich, returned to Lucca. His descendants now live mostly in the cities of São Paulo, San Francisco, and Lucca.

Father to ten children—some of them like my grandfather Delfo, born in Brazil, but the others born in Italy—Egisto was one of those pioneers who ventured across the world at the end of the nineteenth century in search of new opportunities. At the time, Italy was going through an unprecedented economic crisis, exporting manpower to the Americas in impressive numbers, especially to the United States, Brazil, and Argentina.

My research at the Immigration Museum of São Paulo was at first disappointing, because there was no record of Egisto Betti's arrival in Brazil. Some relatives had already tried to obtain information and had given up. The search in the computerized system of the museum did not find his name in the records of any of the ships that arrived in Brazil in the late 1800s, leaving us with a gap in knowledge about the first great adventurer in our family.

In my second attempt, talking with the employee responsible for searching for names in the system, I suggested that he seek just the surname Betti in the database. That was how I identified the entry of a certain "Egicto Betti, from Lucca, 21 years of age, in September 28, 1885, traveling alone on the steamboat *Matteo Bruzzo*." It was him! I had found my great-grandfather! With so much coincidental data, it had to be him! Even the name spelled incorrectly has an explanation: the *s* pronounced with a Tuscan accent could easily have induced the clerk to error, mistaking the *s* for a *c* and resulting in the mysterious *Egicto* that no one had detected before.

You can imagine my excitement at this discovery. The story of my great-grandfather began to take shape. The fragments gradually came together so I could better understand the personality of this courageous man who came alone to Brazil at age twenty-one.

Going up the marble steps of the house he built, I could not help noticing the iron arabesque that flanked the stairway, with emphasis on the initials *E. B.* (Egisto Betti). Within these walls were the remnants of the wealth accumulated by an immigrant who, although he had died young at fifty-eight, had consolidated a large family and returned to his beloved Lucca, leaving as an inheritance his love of Brazil, even stated on his tombstone, which contains the words:

Col sudato sapiente lavoro nel Brasile ospitale,
onorò la patria lontana.
(With his wise and sweaty work in the Brazil that welcomed him,
he honored his distant nation.)

When I saw these words for the first time in 1997, I realized that I was witnessing there the epilogue of an intense life, one based on an unlikely exchange between two countries far apart geographically but very close from the cultural point of view. I identified immediately with the story of this man, who built his future in an unconventional way, managing to differentiate himself from the majority.

Since then, I had been reflecting a lot on the steps I took and the direction I should follow, maturing slowly the idea of returning one day to Lucca and completing a mission begun in 1885 by my great-grandfather. The moment arrived with my return, like the prodigal son, to the house. Like my great-grandfather, I went to see the world, and I learned that one of the main ingredients in the formula for success is the ability to dare.

Without exception, all the stories recounted in this book have that in common; they are stories of people who had the courage to face the unknown, overcoming obstacles and often changing direction as they satisfied the urge to grow, learn, and become better professionals.

The MBA program, for them, was the catalyst to their dreams of progress, and was also a life-changing experience, just as it was for me. Nowadays, instead of being a frustrated and dissatisfied doctor, I am an accomplished man, who tries to convey his experience to younger people and show them new possibilities.

I sincerely hope that these stories, concluded with great satisfaction under the generous Tuscan sun, serve as inspiration to other bold young people who are looking to find their path. I assure you, it is worth it.